REAL ESTATE SMART

The New Home Buying Guide

MATT PARKER

The information, techniques, views, data, and practices in this book do not represent those of the author's or publisher's professional associates, including employers. This publication is designed to provide competent, reliable information regarding the topics covered. However, it is sold with the understanding that the author and publisher are not offering any professional service and/or professional advice, including legal, accounting, financial, health, and fitness. Laws and practices often vary from state to state, and if expert assistance is required, a competent professional should be sought for any legal, accounting, financial, health, and fitness services.

No warranty is made with respect to the accuracy of the information contained herein, and both the author and the publisher specifically disclaim any responsibility for any liability, loss, or risk, personal or otherwise, that is incurred as a consequence, directly or indirectly, from the use and application of any contents in this publication. The author and publisher are not responsible for any third-party websites.

This publication is not medical advice. Please consult a medical or health professional before you begin any nutrition, health, healing, or exercise program, or if you have questions about your health and/or fitness. If you choose to participate in any activity from this book, you do so of your own free will and accord knowingly and voluntarily, assuming all risks associated with such activities.

Performance data and techniques in this book, in addition to laws and regulations, change over time and with respect to location, which could change the status of the information in this book. Past results do not guarantee future performance or results. No information, technique, or plan in this book can or will guarantee any results.

INTRODUCTION

There are known knowns. These are things we know that we know. There are known unknowns. That is to say, there are things that we know we don't know. However, there are also unknown unknowns. There are things we don't know we don't know.

—**DONALD RUMSFELD**

I wish somebody had told me that!
—**ANYONE WHO HAS EVER BOUGHT A HOME**

When you buy a home, the things that "you don't know you don't know" have a profound effect on your life—not just on your financial prosperity—but also your fitness, health, safety, romance, job performance, and happiness.

Consider these facts:

—One feature in a given neighborhood encourages fitness up to 20 percent greater than others.

—One item on your street will make your children significantly safer, particularly from automobile accidents.

—A particular condition you may practice in your home makes many women chronically stressed.

—One trait of your neighbor plays a large part in whether or not you will divorce.

—One decision when signing your loan paperwork can cost you $100,000 or more.

Your distinct personal home choice influences every subsequent decision you make in all of the important categories of your life: love, freedom, influence, and vitality. Your home, including its location, is an inanimate physical construct. Despite this fact, this brick and mortar affects the outcome of your life more than any other physical object you will ever encounter. The real-estate market, as a whole, is far less meaningful to you than your specific location within it.

This book will reveal your distinct personal answers to the following vital questions:

1. How do I maximize the romantic, financial, and interpersonal aspects of my relationship through my home choice?
2. How do I keep my loved ones safe, healthy, and brimming with positive memories?
3. What simple home choices increase my wealth and move me to financial well-being and toward financial freedom?
4. How do I choose a home that makes high-level fitness, physique, confidence, and health natural by-products of my day-to-day life?
5. Which home choice improves my performance at work and places me among positive, productive, and financially exemplary people?

These are the first of many vital housing choices—small, simple choices—you will explore in this book. Once you have applied your personal preference to modern, scientific, and proven housing decision making, you are well equipped to build your best life in the best home for you.

The laws of real-estate past do not apply today; we are fundamentally different than we were even one generation ago:

—Our relationships are increasingly forged through proactive independent choices, as opposed to dependent circumstantial necessity. Who, why, and where we live with has changed.

—Our jobs change frequently, their locations and hours dictated by technology. The job we have in two years may not exist today. The physical location of our job is always in flux.

—Our access to food and health information is unprecedented, yet the complexity of personal nourishment and health care leaves the majority of Americans less energized, less mobile, and less fit.

—Ours is the first American generation expected to live shorter lives than our parents. Does our home motivate fitness, create health, and ensure longevity?

The laws our parents dutifully followed when buying homes have changed. At the time of print, the Case-Shiller Index, the standard time-tested measure for home-value appreciation, shows real-estate price appreciation at just over 0 percent over the last ten years: no increase (over the last thirty years, 1.3 percent increase per year)[1]. Which emotionally instilled laws of generations past do we follow, and what new ones must we learn?

Here is how to be real estate smart.

---

1 US national index levels, not seasonally adjusted. Historic prices are inflation adjusted May 2015 dollars. Dec. 1, 1984 to Dec. 1, 2014.

CONTENTS

SECTION I

HOW A HOUSE HELPS YOUR HEALTH

SECTION II

THE RELATIONSHIP RAMIFICATIONS OF REAL ESTATE

SECTION III

THE FINANCIAL SCIENCE OF SQUARE FOOTAGE

REAL ESTATE SMART

The New Home Buying Guide

SECTION I
HOW A HOUSE HELPS
YOUR HEALTH

Smoking is indispensable if one has nothing to kiss.

—SIGMUND FREUD

Sigmund Freud was born in a rented room in this
locksmith's house, in Příbor, Czech Republic.

1

YOUR ROMANTIC
RELATIONSHIP WITH YOUR
MATERIAL POSSESSIONS

You have a distinct attractive relationship with every material item you own. The strength of the relationship and your emotional intensity toward each item is directly correlated to how much you touch the possession and how long you own it.[1]

Material Item. You have a real emotional bond with your material possessions.

This is one reason smartphones are so dear to us: you touch yours thousands of times a day and develop a real, clinically measurable attachment to it.

This is also a main reason you can't throw away the dozens of old clothing items you haven't worn and will not ever wear again; you are emotionally attached to them. This is because we have direct physical contact with our clothes; they are very difficult to get rid of. How would you feel if someone tried to light your high-school football jersey or favorite T-shirt on fire in front of you?

You probably wouldn't appreciate it!

---

1 James R. Wolf, Hal R. Arkes, and Waleed A. Muhanna, "The Power of Touch: An Exam-ination of the Effect of Duration of Physical Contact on the Valuation of Objects," Judgment and Decision Making 3, no. 6 (August 2008): 476–82.

Human beings have real one-sided attachment feelings for inanimate material objects: we hold precious feelings for things that cannot ever love us back. This is not true for any other species on earth.

The average American domestic unit likely has five hundred to one thousand material possessions in each room of their home. Just go open your drawers to test this fact! American families have in excess of five thousand material possessions in their entire homes, to each of which at least one member of the family probably has some level of emotional connection.

Think about the number of friends you have who have rooms in their homes that contain nothing. You probably can't think of one. In fact, the concept of an empty room seems asocial, weird. When human beings have domestic space, they put things in that space, regardless of whether or not the space, or the things in it, are ever used—if you have space, you will fill it. Every "thing" you put in a space in your home creates a small emotional relationship with that "thing."

Think of owning "things" as having little "friends" who can give you no emotional exchange. The more material things you have, the more small emotional relationships you have. This is why imagining a house fire seems diabolical (a house fire in which none of your actual loved ones are harmed); you will lose thousands of little friends you have small emotional relationships with.

A DYSFUNCTIONAL ANT FARM

—Over nine out of ten, about 92 percent, of American workers are working forty to sixty hours a week.[2] This means we are spending 34–51 percent of our adult working lives working, not including commuting.

—Seventy percent of American workers hate their jobs.[3] So 70 percent of us hate what we spend about one-half of our life doing!

—These same workers (us) are using the resources from our jobs to buy homes where we store over five thousand material possessions we develop relationships with but cannot provide any emotion in return.

—Time actually spent at home, the location we pay for and fill with material things, continues to decrease.

This sounds like a population of insane entities. **The consumption/stockpile method does not work for us; it makes us stressed, burdened, and detached from our peers.**

Seen from space, our planet is a blue-and-green ant farm in a black abyss. If gods looked down upon the scurrying masses of activity, the vast majority of Americans would appear to be feverishly working to collect and stockpile disposable items. Again, no other animal does this. It is a function of our human emotional programming.

Have you ever seen any bird nest or dog house in which an animal crowded itself out with any objects? There exists no example of such behavior. We are the only living things that build, then subsequently overcrowd, the individual space in which we live with disposable items.

In extreme cases, some people, hoarders, actually store enough material possessions to render their homes unlivable and unsafe. Some humans actually render their personal space unfit for safe, healthy residence. This is ironic, given that we buy homes to be safe.

2 Based on Gallup data from the 2013 and 2014 Work and Education polls. http://www.gallup.com/poll/175286/hour-workweek-actually-longer-seven-hours.aspx.

3 Gallup 2013 State of the American Workplace. http://www.ryot.org/gallup-poll-70-americans-disengaged-jobs/376177.

IS THIS UNHEALTHIER FOR
MALE OR FEMALE ANTS?

If you have space, you will fill it with things which you will become emotionally attached to. This is a nearly infallible statement; I challenge you to find a significant space in your home, or a friend's, that is void of material items. There exists a tipping point when your seemingly benign "storage" turns to clutter, disorganization, and crowding, and **it has strong negative health effects on the female matron in your household.**[4]

Clutter makes women sick. In fact, research shows that this collection of items and clutter causes us real stress, the level and type of which contributes to chronic ailment and disease; sleep disorders, sexual impotence, high blood pressure, heart disease, and cancer. If you live in a hurricane path of clutter and disorganization in your home, it is very likely making the matron of your domestic unit sick, emotionally and physically.

As a people, we are increasingly distracted from tangible human conversation yet emotionally bonding to a collection of material items created in foreign communities. *The average couple spends about one and one and half hours shopping for goods or services per day.*[5] How much time do you spend with your partner without any distraction per day? Do you spend more time shopping every day than you spend in uninterrupted engagement with your partner? It would be hard for someone to make the argument that this vast collection of material items is enhancing our health, relationships, and scholarly pursuits.

This chapter should prompt you to consider how much space you want in a home to fill with plastic items you will have emotional feelings for. Additionally, it should lead you to consider the current clutter condition of your residence. If there is a room, or rooms, in your home that you use less than an hour a week, is it/are they worth having? The next time you buy, how big of a home will you buy?

The more nonfunctional, unimportant square footage you have in your home, the more trite relationships you and your family will have with your

4 Jeanne E. Arnold et al., Life at Home in the Twenty-First Century: 32 Families Open Their Doors (Los Angeles, CA: The Cotsen Institute of Archaeology Press, July 12, 2012).

5 US Bureau of Labor Statistics, "American Time Use Survey, 2014 Results," published June 24, 2015.

little friends, your vast collection of disposable plastic items. What's worse, in exchange for this relationship, you and your loved ones will all give up an important allocation of your most valuable possession...

...Time.

The True Cost of Material Items

If our lives were endless, if we lived forever, these topics would be far less important. Obviously, we do not live forever. You will fill underutilized space in your home with things. This requires time, your only true irreplaceable resource. Underutilized space in your home represents an expenditure of time, more than money.

To think of the material items in your home as only having a purchase price is inaccurate. In other words, a lounge chair doesn't just "cost" you what you paid for it—let's say $900. There are at least eleven other potential costs to actually owning the lounge chair:

Time:
1. One hour (minimum)—shopping for, and buying, new lounge chair.
2. Returning time—a certain percentage of your purchases will be returned, requiring time.
3. Disposal time—time it takes to eventually get rid of the lounge chair.

Emotional:
4. Emotional feeling of loss if lounge chair is stained or ruined.
5. Emotional energy considering disposal of lounge chair.
6. Emotional energy actually disposing of the lounge chair. (If you've ever tried to get rid of a piano, you know exactly what I am talking about!).

Financial:
7. Purchase price.
8. Money spent on traveling to multiple stores to find the right lounge chair.
9. Money spent storing the lounge in real estate—you are paying for the space where it rests.

10. Money spent on energy and resources to clean and wash the lounge chair.
11. Money spent on ultimate disposal (selling or giving away) of lounge chair—resources spent driving to disposal place.

All of the costs above can be translated into time: either time itself, emotions translated into time, or time spent earning money to actualize the above—*a lounge chair doesn't just cost you money, it costs you an allotment of time*. The time devoted to the lounge chair is irreplaceable and priceless by definition.

Given enough time, you will always be able to earn more money. No amount of money, though, will guarantee you more time.

When you buy something, from a simple purchase to a house, you should be considering if it is worth the time. The true monetary "price" of any item is not a reflection of its impact on your life. Any object you purchase requires more than just a one-time financial payment. This is immediately, perhaps surprisingly, evident when you buy your first home.

When you buy a home, you should consider how much space— square footage—you want to fill with time, not just how much it costs or how much you can afford.

WHAT DOES YOUR SPACE IN THE ANT FARM LOOK LIKE?

The trend for American workers is to spend three decades erecting a disposable castle:

In our thirties, we save and toil to buy homes.

In our forties, we maintain and use them.

In our fifties, we improve them to sell, so that we can move into smaller homes with better views in better neighborhoods. After having successfully worked for, and owned, a large home, people tend to buy a smaller one. If more space meant more happiness, people would upsize later in life when they had more money. They do not, we do not. We do the opposite after learning the lesson over two to three decades.

How much of your time in these three decades of your life do you want to devote to physical space that stores inanimate objects? How much of your time do you want to dedicate to family, vocation, vacation, and health?

As emotional animals, we form relationships. A clear shortcoming of this wonderful emotional capacity is that it does not end with things that give us emotional interchange back; it extends to plastic and all things not alive. To maximize your important relationships, you need time. And, time is what you devote to extra square footage that you fill with your little plastic friends.

SMALL NEW CONSTRUCTION

Most people choose to buy resale homes, as opposed to build new construction because it is far easier and requires far less liquid cash.

Building new construction requires either cash or a loan for the duration of the building project. The down payments for these loan programs and their interest rates are far less favorable than conforming to residential resale mortgage rates.

It's really expensive to build a new home.

Currently, as a general rule of thumb, construction loans are granted when the value of the structure to be built is worth twice what the lot is worth. You could get a $300,000 new-construction loan in a circumstance where your lot was valued at about $100,000, and the home itself, the physical residence, would be worth about $200,000. It would be difficult, if not impossible in most places, to get a standard construction loan, in this case, if the home (the structure portion of the real estate) to be built were only going to be worth $100,000.

For this reason, among others, the square footage of homes is dictated by banks' preference to loan at these ratios: it is really only possible for you, and builders, to build conforming home sizes. If you want to build a relatively small home, under ordinary circumstances in the current lending environment, it's really not an option if you want a loan. Nor is it an attractive or viable option for builders to build smaller homes.

2

WHAT DISNEYLAND AND "GO AWAY GREEN" TEACH US ABOUT THE BEST COLOR

Disney theme parks release almost one bug per visitor per year in their parks. Walt Disney World Resort, Florida, is said to have let loose at least ten million bugs into their park in a given year.

Have you ever been bitten by a bug at a Disney Park?

Have you ever seen a fly at a Disney Park?

Probably not. Despite being some of the biggest gardens in the country, Disney Theme Parks are devoid of pests. They practice sophisticated ecosystem management, including the release of "beneficial" bugs in their landscapes, to maintain the most magical gardens in the world.

Disney is said to have concocted a particular shade of green paint, "Go Away Green," for the man-made parts of their parks to make them blend into the landscape. No matter how many times you go to a Disney Park, and no matter how hard you look, it is nearly impossible to see the nuts and bolts of their theme ride engineering behind their prolific gardening.

In fact, the first thing you see upon entering one of Disney's signature theme parks is Mickey Mouse created of blooming flowers that get replanted six to ten times a year adhering to scrupulous standards. It is impossible to imagine Disneyland without landscaping. It would be like seeing a body without flesh and skin, just bones.

Disney is as much a horticultural marvel as it is a roller coaster park. One of their most important competitive advantages is knowledge of an affliction that you have.

DO YOU HAVE BIOPHILIA?

All other things being equal, would you take a home with a water view, or one without a water view?

If the windows of your home could look toward concrete buildings or green foliage, which would you take?

Imagine, for a second, Disneyland without any foliage, flowers, or fauna of any kind. Would it feel the same?

The majority of people, including children, have been tested to prefer the more natural of each of these cases; water views, green views, and lush landscaping. What's more, simple natural additions to your environment have profound, noticeable effects on your physical and emotional health.

Biophilia means "craving life." The biophilia hypothesis is the idea that human beings are drawn to natural environments, views, and phenomena because nature is where our species originated. Stated simply—people prefer natural things to unnatural things.

Consider the following:

—Your children are less likely to be hit by a car on a tree-lined street. People who live on tree-lined streets drive slower in their own neighborhoods, and their streets experience slower traffic and less traffic accidents.[1]

—Your small business makes 20 percent more sales with the presence of a significant number of mature trees.[2]

—You experience lower postwork stress with a more landscaped (greener) yard. People who live in homes with treed landscapes and green window views burn off the stress of their days faster than those who do not.

1 Dan Burden, 22 Benefits of Urban Street Trees (Glatting Jackson, Walkable Communities, November 2008). http://www.michigan.gov/documents/dnr/22_benefits_208084_7.pdf.

2 Ibid.

—Multifamily buildings with trees lower the occurrence rate of domestic violence.[3]

—Even brief encounters with nature improve your capacity to concentrate.[4]

—Mature adults and elderly people live longer in greener neighborhoods.[5]

—Green areas near your home give you healthier breathable air, more comfortable temperatures to live and play in and generally better environs to be fit, smart, and productive.[6]

—Tree-lined streets are 10–20 percent cooler in the summer than streets without mature tree growth. The same tree-lined streets are warmer than streets without trees in the winter.

Human beings find almost instantaneous peace and happiness through exposure to nature. This is a result of biophilia and why Disneyland has award winning landscaping. If you stop to imagine your most restful, refreshing, and joyful places, they probably have a distinct natural aspect to them.

So, people in greener neighborhoods are safer; their small businesses more successful; they are more relaxed, kinder, live longer; and they are more productive. This sounds like a neighborhood most people would want to live in! But what about people who don't have the option of living in a lush, green neighborhood?

Not everyone can afford a view or living in a tree-lined street!

The prescription for nature, for green, for serene, is so small that you can manufacture it wherever you live and/or work. **This is a cost-effective wonder drug of which you need only a sip.**

The simple addition of one plant, one single plant, has been shown to have immense physiological and physical healing effects on hospital patients. One little plant! Here are some ideas to assuage your biophilia and

3 Kuo and W. C. Sullivan, "Aggression and Violence in the Inner City: Impacts of Environment Via Mental Fatigue," Environment & Behavior 33, no. 4 (2001): 543–71.

4 R. Kaplan and S. Kaplan, The Experience of Nature: A Psychological Perspective (Cambridge: Cambridge University Press, 1989).

5 Ibid

6 K. Tzoulas et al., "Promoting Ecosystem and Human Health in Urban Areas Using Green Infrastructure: A Literature Review," Landscape and Urban Planning 81 (2007): 167–78.

maximize the free happy pills nature offers:

—Pay attention to the rooms you spend your time in and where the windows look. Can you pick a home with aesthetically better kitchen views, or can you create aesthetic views from your kitchen using affordable landscaping?

—Can you create natural walls outside your windows using bamboo, hanging plants, and other inexpensive landscaping?

—Does the home you are considering, or the one you have, have options for "high" windows—windows that are positioned high on walls, to avoid looking directly at buildings and instead creating viewing portals to blue sky or green trees? In almost any locale, you can grab the best of outdoors by carefully choosing your windows to frame blue skies or green leaves.

—Does the home you are considering, or the one you have, have opportunity for a natural screen between the home and the street? Can you erect a low maintenance fence that encourages flowing vines?

—Can you easily place bird feeders strategically around your home?

These considerations are vital in a developing atmosphere that lends itself to large, simple, homogeneous neighborhoods devoid of mature plant life. Humans, you included, have biophilia. For maximal physical, emotional, and relationship health, you do need minimal exposure to the tangible world that you were born of.

This is not a value judgment against modern development, neighborhoods, or city living. It is a collection of bona fide data that should remind you to maximize your exposure to naturally aesthetic features, heaven created, or manufactured and propagated by you. All of us have daydreamed and considered hiding in Disneyland and staying there full time, but there are simpler, safer ways to incorporate the free gifts of small, live, additions to your daily routines.

3

LOCATION, LOCATION, LOCATION.
FITNESS, FITNESS.

The CrossFit gym in Burien, Washington, located between SeaTac Airport and Puget Sound south of Seattle, thrusts hot air into your face when you open its door in the summer. The cinder-block structure stands as a lonely soldier in a lake of black asphalt on a prominent corner in the quaint Americana Olde Towne portion of Burien. Nine months a year, it's a comfortable place to recreate. June through August, however, the gym turns into a human pizza oven. These months you can often find someone throwing up in the street outside the front doors, having both been sufficiently and simultaneously whipped and cooked during the course of a sweaty workout.

The gym gets really, really hot three months a year.

On a particularly sweltering summer day in 2012, I unlocked the door for a 6:00 a.m. workout. It was already hot enough to melt your shoes inside. I realized, again, that I should have negotiated air conditioning in the lease that I and two other founding members of the gym signed for the business. I walked through the gym toward the back door so I could start to ventilate the large microwave to a temperature that actually allowed me to breathe.

On the way to the back service door, I tripped over a sleeping bag. The primary founding partner and head coach was actually sleeping in the gym. Our shoestring budget had forced the former collegiate boxer into living on a Therm-a-Rest and drawing water from an industrial sink. This guy was committed.

He was not only dedicated but he was also the finest performing athlete and physical specimen I had ever met. In fact, one day when some of us trekked to Machu Picchu, we were at the crux of the archaeological adventure taking pictures of Huayna Picchu, and a group of female Japanese tourists asked us to take pictures of him. They were at the apex of a timeless, world-class spiritual viewpoint, and the young ladies wanted a picture of my friend!

Discovering he was not only coaching at the gym but also living in it from time to time, I realized my odds of competing with him in CrossFit workouts were the same as the odds of Japanese females taking pictures of me—negligible.

What impact does where you sleep, your home, have on your fitness? If you have an extra five, fifteen, or fifty pounds you have been meaning to lose, a fitter location may be the trick. If fitness is important to you, your partner, your loved ones, and even your pets, your home location is vital. Its location has huge implications with regard to your fitness.

Buying a Strong Home

No inherently simple concept has become more infinitely confused and complicated than fitness. The proliferation of money-making fitness products and services has produced an endless informational galaxy of fitness information that leads to misinformation. This is possible when physical activity is initiated by someone who had been sedentary, which then produces profound tangible results.

For about three months.

Then productivity gains decrease; the average person becomes sedentary again and subsequently is ready for a new fitness fad. It is a predictable, albeit not personally optimal, social cycle. Think of Bowflex, P90X, Bikram Yoga, and even CrossFit. If any of these actually were the golden cow of perfect fitness and health, they wouldn't be routinely replaced with new and different fitness regimes.

Novel fitness plans, protocols, gyms, and media appear daily all around us. As an example, if you sit down to research training for a marathon today, you will find myriad prescriptions so dichotomous that it's possible your research would leave you more rather than less confused about the best plan for training.

One typical winning formula for fitness fads is to take a commonly held practice, reverse it 180 degrees, and insanely suggest the opposite. Then folks try it.

How about running ten miles, on concrete, without shoes, after you haven't run in three years?[1] Running without shoes on man-made surfaces when you have worn shoes every day of your entire life?

Eastern philosophy, including yoga, has taught clear breathing practices for thousands of years. Then people who haven't done more than twenty consecutive minutes of cardiovascular conditioning in a decade actually work out with elevation masks on.

It's easy to see how people will make fun of these in a decade, if they aren't already. The point is that omnipresent fitness information can be confusing at best and injurious at worst.

A glowing green alien, if she existed, might offer the best advice for marathon training after watching several marathons from a cloaked flying saucer in the sky:

Run.

If you have baseline health, and you start running and then keep running, your body will basically direct the training. It will tell you how far to run, when to run, how hard to run, when to rest, what to eat, and when to eat. If at some point during your training you want to take your shoes off and put on an elevation mask, go for it.

For the majority of people training for a marathon, this would be the best, clearest, most action-promoting activity they could to do train for a marathon.

Run.

Fitness is simple.

Health professionals generally prescribe fifteen to thirty minutes of activity per day for a fitness level that will support a healthy body, healthy

---

1 Author's note—Born to Run, by Christopher McDougall, one of the books that prompted and promulgated barefoot running, is a fantastic read. I highly recommend the book. I find it hard to believe, though, that even McDougall has supported unfettered shoeless running on pavement, as many everyday athletes tried. This comment, footnoted from above, is not a "jab" at McDougall or his suggestions and findings. Generally speaking, I agree with his ethos with regard to barefoot running; I just believe that, like any fitness fad, it can be practiced poorly.

mind, and general well-being. Fifteen to thirty minutes per day! This amount of activity is consistently proven to be an absolutely free wonder drug. It causes:

—increased energy and vitality;
—improved physical appearance;
—optimized brain functioning and intellectual focus;
—minimized likelihood of chronic ailments, including heart conditions and diabetes;
—minimized likelihood of nagging temporary ailments like colds and influenza;
—maximized sexual performance and enjoyment; and
—improved interpersonal dynamics and opportunity for meaningful interpersonal connections.

The average person doesn't have to run a marathon a day to see these benefits. They simply have to maintain consistent activity for fifteen to thirty minutes. From a time and financial standpoint, this is, without question, the least costly way to safely and quickly medicate many of your physical and emotional challenges. In the amount of time it takes to watch one episode of The Big Bang Theory, you can alter your entire life's path. Fitness is easy: do something active every day for fifteen to thirty minutes. It doesn't matter whether you are wearing shoes or not.

Your Walkability Score Can Lengthen Your Life

Adults who live in the greenest urban areas are three times more likely to practice fitness than those who live in the least green settings.[2] They're also proven to be healthier.[3]

"Despite the fact that humans have created massive technological landscapes, many cross

2 K. L. Wolf, "Active Living—A Literature in Review," in Green Cities: Good Health (www.greenhealth.washgington.edu) (College of Environment, University of Washington, 2010).

3 J. Maas, et al., "Green Space, Urbanity, and Health: How Strong is the Relation?" Journal of Epidemiology and Community Health 60 (2006): 5897–592.

cultural studies show that we instinctively crave natural features in our surroundings."
—CHARLES A. LEWIS, GREEN NATURE, *HUMAN NATURE.*

The presence of a park within walking distance of your home means you will easily engage in 20 percent more outdoor, fresh-air, active endeavors during the course of your week. A 20 percent increase in fitness, for most people, would be the impetus of weight loss, better appearance, more confidence, decreased health risks, less stress, and better sleep.

The "walkability" score on your home doesn't just mean you will work out more and be healthier. Elderly people actually live longer in more walkable neighborhoods.[4] Homes within about fifteen hundred feet of a public park sell for approximately $4,200 more than homes that are not.[5]

WHAT IS "WALKABLE?"

—Tree-lined streets and/or streets with abundant green landscaping.
—Presence of a park or trails within approximately one thousand feet or less of your home. Or, you can walk to a park within five minutes.
—Presence of sidewalks.

These factors affect elderly and young people more than others. Why does your home location with respect to sidewalks, tree-lined streets, green space, and parks help dictate the quality and length of your life?

DOGS AFFECT MY CHILDREN'S FITNESS?

Human beings are genetically predisposed to pursuing the easiest courses of action available to us. From an evolutionary standpoint, this would have conserved calories for us in a competitive wild environment. For example, if you need creamer for the coffee at your office this morn-

4 T. Takano, K. Nakamura, and M. Watanabe, "Urban Residential Environments and Senior Citizens' Longevity in Mega-City Areas: The Importance of Walkable Green Space," Journal of Epidemiology and Community Health 56, no. 12 (2002): 913–16.

5 Chris Parsons, "Economic Value of Natural Environment: Understanding Washington's Critical Areas," Fish and Wildlife Planner. July 2006. http://wdfw.wa.gov/publications/00665/wdfw00665.pdf.

ing, and it is a five-minute walk or a five-minute car trip including parking, will you walk or drive?

Despite knowing there are many benefits to the walk, personal and social, and desiring to be the person who walks, most people, including me, would drive.

This predisposition for ease has proven a winning formula for the first six million years of human development. Easier options, for the entirety of our development, have basically meant calorie preservation, a major component of survival in the wild.

Difficult, confusing, and uncomfortable options are unattractive to human beings as a species. Overcoming such options requires discipline. Human beings vary in their individual allotment of daily discipline, but unquestionably discipline is a finite resource for everyone on this planet. Every day, you only have so much discipline. At some point, you run out of discipline and revert to easy, predisposed, and habitual actions.

If you are dieting, when do you overeat? Probably late at night, or

THE DOG WALKING THE CHILD
Children with dogs are more active. They are more likely to walk in their neighborhood and play in their yard and in the street.

when you have been drinking—times when your discipline level is low.

Are you more likely to skip a workout early or late in the day? For most people, it's easier to miss a workout late in the day, when the other tasks of the day have required valuable allotments of your discipline.

Do you drive more safely when you are alert, rested, and tranquil or when you are stressed and rushed? In which state are you more likely to start using your smartphone, an unsafe distraction, while driving?

When you have discipline, you make better decisions and act precisely. When you lack discipline, you are more likely to make hasty decisions and act imprecisely.

This is not a law that applies only to certain demographics; it is universal to human beings, from presidents to paupers, and a defining trait of our dramatic history. Given that your daily allotment of discipline is fixed and that it dictates many outcomes in your life, you have the following two options for making better, more specific life-altering decisions:

—Develop higher level of discipline by working at it.
—Make good decisions easy, palatable, and enjoyable.

People make better decisions when the better decision is easy to make. People make poor decisions when the right decision is hard to make.

This is precisely why McDonald's french fries might be the single favorite hot snack food in history. Not only are they really good, but they are really easy to get, inexpensive, and easy to eat.

Someone could make you a great bowl of chicken salad, which would be much healthier, but the time, financial, and functionality costs of eating the chicken salad are all about ten times that of french fries. It takes a lot of discipline to find, pay for, and then sit down and eat any salad.

Putting yourself in a position to make a good decision easily is a powerful way to achieve success in any venture. With regard to your fitness and health, the longevity of your loved ones and pets, you should do your best to make fitness easy, comfortable, and enjoyable.

But we are not talking about one order of McDonald's french fries (which, by the way, are too delicious to ever totally give up) with regard to a home purchase. Where your home is located presents a buffet of simple fitness choices, most of them made subconsciously.

In a relatively short real-estate career of about ten years, I have successfully helped people purchase hundreds of condominiums, homes, lots, and commercial buildings. Not once, in ten years, has anyone ever taken a walk from a property they were in contract to purchase. Not once has someone explored the sidewalk more than approximately one hundred feet from their front door. No one has functionally tested their walkability, but universally they have hired inspectors to tell them if their potential dishwasher works properly.

A walkable neighborhood need not be rich. You don't have to live in a posh suburb or a neighborhood of award winning Leed-certified green homes to maximize your health through your home setting. Nor is this an argument against city living, or condominium ownership; many urban settings were thoughtfully planned by progressive, whole-minded developers and architects. **You simply have to choose, among the options available to you, locations whereby you enjoy walking out the front door.** This seemingly minute detail will probably make you and your loved ones significantly healthier.

Before you ever hire an inspector to determine the polarity of a fourteen-dollar electrical socket, take your dog for a walk in your potential new neighborhood. This will tell you more, without any thinking, than any report can provide. You are looking for sidewalks, parks, green spaces, generally landscaped environments, and enjoyable outdoor spaces. The preciseness of these things, and the feelings they create, will subconsciously encourage your health to a very significant degree.

WALKING UP?

If you leave the front door of your home for a walk, do you walk up (increase elevation)?

If you buy a home where this is the case, two trends are likely to occur. First, you will not enjoy walking from your home as much. If you have to walk up to start a walk from your home, the real energy needed to start is significant! As you probably know, simply starting any activity is the most difficult part—"starting the engine." Once you get going, your body and breathing patterns sync, and activity takes on a sort of natural flow. However, starting is generally the toughest part of physical activity.

If you have to walk up to start a walk from your house, it is less likely you will engage in the basic activity of walking from your

Homes placed above grade are optimal not only from an aesthetic and but also from a fitness standpoint; they encourage you to walk and recreate, because they are easy to walk from (down).

house.

Second, buyers prefer homes you drive up to. That is to say, from the street, people and/or their cars enter your property and then gently move up in elevation to get to the house, garage, and front door.

Try to think of any popular public building, now or in the past, in which civilians walk down to get to the entrance. You probably can't think of many, if any at all. People tend to prefer going up when they approach a building (more on why this may be the case in chapter 6, "Waterfront or War Front"). When you buy a home, consider this fact. It will make your home more enjoyable to approach and easier to sell.

4

WHICH OF YOUR FIVE SENSES IS THE MOST IMPORTANT TO HEED WHEN BUYING A HOME?

Carson Johnson, my childhood best friend, had a backyard that hosted many of our sporting events. If you hit a home run to the west, into the woods above the Puget Sound, the outfielder rarely came out of the foliage empty-handed; he almost always found the ball, and we resumed play.

A home run to the right, or a foul ball, landed easily in my grumpy grandfather's apple orchard; you only risked his gruff rants on that side. We found almost all Wiffle balls, footballs, and soccer balls we banged into the orchard.

However, any foul ball hit to the south was a missing plane in the Bermuda triangle. The left fielder or the third baseman might take a cursory look into the ivy at the foot of the woods there, but that was all. Inevitably, he would say, "That one's gone; grab a new ball guys," with a slight shiver of fear in his voice.

We would complain for a moment, call the third baseman a baby, and maybe even yell at him, "We're running out of Wiffle balls, you sissy! Get in there and get it!"

However, you never pushed too hard, never really pressed the third baseman to go into the woods. The second he even walked toward the black wall of dripping ivy-cloaked fir trees, you got goose bumps on the outside of your forearms. At an unknown distance into the living woods to the south, the left side of the baseball diamond, there was haunted house.

If you took more than one step into the woods on that side of the field, the sun blacked out, the birds stopped singing, and an invisible evil magnet seemed to pull at your cotton T-shirt, beckoning you deeper into a childhood nightmarish black ravine. It was far more palatable to ask your mom to take you to Fred Meyer for a new pack of Wiffle balls than it was to risk falling into a tangle of musty, dark ivy that could wrap you up and pull you to a hellish haunted mansion.

THE HOUSE WITH AN ORGAN IN ITS WALLS

My childhood friend Carson is now a pilot who lives with his family in Minneapolis, Minnesota. He grew up in a densely wooded high-bank waterfront lot south of Seattle, Washington. Nestled privately about one hundred feet above the shores of Puget Sound, his front yard was functionally over fifteen acres of dense, ivy-covered fir trees, swampy streams, and screeching eagles. In the summer, we could leave his home, large Mr. Freeze treats in our hands, and journey into a Narnia-esque child's playground for the better part of any day.

There was so much wooded space because my friend's home and lot abutted a large parcel, a ravine, which hid what we believed to be a historic early twentieth-century bootlegger mansion. It was over eight thousand feet big (more than five times the average US home size), without road or trail access, and covered with dense vegetation; the home still presents an eerie ghost-brushed glow under the deep shade of all the 150-foot fir trees around it.

The bootlegger mansion, still standing, has two wings: a housing wing and a music hall. The music hall rivals a basketball court in size. At one end of it, there is a fireplace big enough to walk into, standing up. In fact, the seating for the fireplace actually gives the edge to it, terracing back upward to the rest of the music hall. You could almost fit a Prius in the fireplace.

In the ceiling of the hall, there are hundreds of wood panels, each one of them roughly the size of a shoebox. The panels are obviously disconnected from each other at their borders; there's a good amount of space visible between them. Each panel can be moved to redirect sound emanating from an organ actually built into the walls of the expansive room.

It is the single most interesting room in any home I have seen on the west coast. You will never see it when driving by, from a boat, or even from a helicopter or drone. Even bushwhacking to the home by foot will land you in the hospital (if not in jail!). For being within twenty minutes of downtown Seattle, it's also the most private urban setting I have ever experienced.

The only evidence of the home, for decades now, has been the sound.

As children, we never actually got close enough to the home to touch it. To our knowledge, no one lived there. We only had stories of ghostly, strong organ music belting out from a dense stand of suburban forest. Every time we got close enough to the mansion to look in, the hair on the back of our necks stood straight up. All it took was a bird rustling in the bushes to set one of us, then the other, into a dead sprint home. There was probably a pile of Mr. Freeze wrappers near the home, recording our closest approach to the home.

Within the last twenty years, the home has changed hands several times. One of the owners was a prominent Seattle-area musician. When he owned it, members of Pearl Jam, Soundgarden, and Alice'N Chains used the home to "jam" in. When I listed a home for sale adjacent to this one but separated by acres of forest, I got a wide range of opinions about hearing the jam sessions, which would fill the lower part of a neighborhood with professional-level rock music.

"I can't stand that music interrupting my weekends!"

I would hear this from five to ten people. Another handful of people would tell me:

"How cool it is that we get to hear live music of that talent level!"

Indeed, the opinions with regard to the value of the music were highly varied and clearly subjective. This is true of all noise—whether it bothers you or not can be largely subjective. **The problem is that sound is the most important of your five features to heed when considering a home, and it's not common for buyers to test sound at a home during the buying process.**

No one—and no real-estate website metric—can truly predict your personal physical response to any sound. To me, crashing waves might be crashing cars; the constant, thundering rhythm of wave action, despite my passion for watersports, leaves me tossing in my sleep for hours, and subsequently I wake up eager to jog away from the noise.

But many people love sleeping near the sound of waves. Waves, though, would obviously be thundering, and thus evident, round the clock at any home you were considering.

What about other noises, though? Music, from musicians or a church? Airplane noise? Traffic noise? Barking dogs?

Some variations of these are audible at all hours, but most sounds emanate intermittently. The majority of these noises are unlikely to be heard for one or two hours at any home. When you move in, though, you will definitely hear them, and some of these noises do create chronic frustration.

What some consider a private, professional concert on a weekend, leaves others calling their attorneys.

HOW DOES NOISE CAUSE BIRTH DEFECTS?

By definition, noise is something you can hear. There are definitely positive noises, experienced in positive levels: light wind, light rain, and certain types of music. But the wrong types of noise, in the wrong levels, cause vastly more physical human problems then you may know.

Noise is the hardest thing to remediate in a home and neighborhood, many times impossible to remediate. Noise is also the most physically harmful thing in any neighborhood, short of a rare poisonous environmental contaminant (arsenic, for example, in your soil.).

Hearing is a primary sense that you cannot turn off at night; all other senses you can. Additionally, "white noise" is somewhat a myth: you may consciously forget about a sound, but your brain still hears and deals with that noise subconsciously. Prolonged exposure to noise, even what we call "background noise," has drastic negative effects on your life.

Bad noise has been proven to cause the following:

—birth defects
—violence
—decreased learning and information retention and memory
—impatience
—sleep problems
—heart problems

—ulcers
—migraines

Noise, from a biological standpoint, triggers a stress response that was very helpful to us as a developing species; reacting to noise meant survival. Now, there are myriad sources of community noise where you may be choosing to live. Take a moment and think about the best nights of sleep you have had. Universally, they tend to evoke quiet, relaxed memories of peaceful rooms.

So far, we've considered two different types of sounds: (1) sounds that may be subjectively positive or negative, preferred or scorned, and (2) background noises that cause real, physically harmful problems.

Both forms of sound can and should be considered when you choose your next residence, but you must take the time to find them. Take multiple trips to your next home at different times before you make a decision that will keep you there for years. Tell your real estate agent to be quiet and your children to play, and you sit down in the kitchen. Lie down where you will be sleeping. Open the window where your office will be.

What can you hear?

Check for sounds and persistent background noise that bother you. Both of these will cause poorer mental and physical health for you and your family. How would you feel if you saved for twenty years to buy a view home and then realized you were next to a performing music venue, like the haunted mansion? Some people really like it. For others, it would ruin the purchase to the point of selling the home they just bought.

What about airplane noise or noise from an active train track? These are thundering examples of what folks call "white noise." You probably won't subconsciously get used to these sounds, but they can and do cause severe health problems, either in large doses or in persistent doses.

HIPPIES WITH HEARING AIDS

Sounds are the only regular external factors to your home, again, excluding rare environmental contaminants, which will actually make you impotent, emotionally stressed, and chronically sick. Anything you see will not do this; you control what you taste and feel, and you can shut your doors to smells. Loud sounds, and persistent sounds, will either damage your health, or force you to move. No regular sight or smell will do the same.

Just ask the residents near Coupeville, on Whidbey Island, Washington, who live near Naval Air Station Whidbey Island. They recently filed a motion for an injunction in US District Court to make the US Navy stop using a local airstrip for simulated aircraft carrier takeoffs, landings, and touchdowns. Apparently, the citizens of the bucolic island town were suffering severely from the practice:

"They're suffering hypertension, increased blood pressure, cardiac events such as arrhythmias, increased diabetes, gastrointestinal problems, depression, anxiety, sleep disorders, hearing loss, tinnitus," according to their attorney, Ken Pickard.[1]

This particular case is far from over, but the debate about the effects of harmful sounds is not. Again, harmful sounds either are those that bother you personally or the persistent background noises. The sounds don't have to be navy jets to be harmful; they can be the simple hum of a freeway, the persistent barking of dogs, the constant rattle of construction, or any noise that adversely affect you. Pay attention to your hearing, above all else, before you argue with your spouse about which counter tops look the best.

1 From "Battle over Navy Jet Noise on Whidbey Island Pits Neighbor Against Neighbor," on mynorthwest. com, April 29, 2015. http://mynorthwest.com/11/2754540/Battle-over-Navy-jet-noise-on-Whidbey-Island-pits-neighbor-against-neighbor.

5

IS THE MOST IMPORTANT VIEW OUTSIDE OR INSIDE?

Without a doubt, the overconsumption of television and passive electronic entertainment make your children unsafely overweight, intellectually less capable, and socially less intelligent. More than one to two hours of television and gaming-type activities, outside of school, per day, is proven to be severely detrimental to your children. Additionally, given the universal interconnected nature of electronic devices, the types of media your children are consuming are varied and uncontrolled; not only is overconsumption of media unhealthy, it can be degrading to your family values.

Two housing features can go a long way to alleviating these challenges.

If you've been camping around chipmunks, you know they will instantly find *any* food you give them a chance to get to! If you leave a small opening in a bag of tortilla chips, even the size of a Tic Tac, any resident chipmunk will seek out the bag and tear it open with feverous energy, inviting its brothers to indulge in a waterfall of chips.

Any piece of food, any crumb, you drop, draws chipmunks immediately to your feet. Some chipmunks will even scamper up on your shoes to satiate their desire for sweet or salty human food. In the worst case, if you ate a doughnut just before retiring to sleep in your tent at night, and you left crumbs on your clothing, you may wake up with a tiny scampering chipmunk on your chest.

Campground chipmunks are professional food-scrap collectors.

Your children are professional media consumers.

Between televisions, computers, and smart devices, there really is no end to the cartoons and media your children can find and ingest. Your children are undiscerning, like the chipmunks, with regard to what they consume and how much they consume. **If they can find passive entertainment easily, they will consume it.** This would include smartphones. Americans have five to fifteen "crumbs" of media in their homes; these are all easy places for your children to find and consume any media they want.

Unless you can keep the media in a sealed bag.

Imagine two homes, both with eight rooms in total:

Imagine the first with five televisions—one in the living room, one in each of three bedrooms, and one in the garage.

Imagine the other has two televisions: one in the living room adjoining the kitchen and one in the master suite.

In the first home, the one with five televisions in five different rooms, your children have five places they can play hide and seek with you. If you tell them to turn off a television in the living room, they can operate around your commandment by going to a bedroom with a television. If you walk to this bedroom to tell them to turn off the TV, they can still head outside, reenter the garage, and watch TV again.

As you can see, in this case, limiting television consumption is exhaustive!

Now let's go to the second home, the one with two televisions, the nicest of which would be in the kitchen area. If you are like the average American, you spend approximately one-half of your waking hours at home in your kitchen. In this case, it's easy to monitor television.

Additionally, not only can you monitor the *amount* of television they watch, you can also supervise *what* they are watching while you carry on living your life in the kitchen. Herein is the first key to keeping your chipmunks healthy: dictate the type and amount of media they are able to consume by placing the media devices in the kitchen and the rooms immediately adjoining the kitchen. Limit electronic devices that your children have immediate access to these locations.

The case is not being made that adults should suffer this dearth of televisions. Children generally don't retreat to your master suite, and you will have a television island for yourself in there; there's still a television in your bedroom you can secure from your children.

The second key to keeping your chipmunks healthy from a media-consumption standpoint is living in an open floor plan. Parents with open floor plans report a significantly greater level of control over their children's television consumption. An open floor plan is generally defined as a kitchen, living room area, and dining area that can all be easily seen to and from each other.

Open floor plans are popular currently, and they generally feel spacious, roomy, and bright. *Besides being bright, modern, stylish, and generally comfortable, they provide a much more important feature: open visual and verbal communication.* With an open floor plan, your team is always in a huddle, as opposed to spread out all over the field.

Line of sight from the kitchen to the rooms adjoining it is vital to easily monitoring your children's behavior, and the behavior of the children they are interacting with. If you are worried about television consumption in your home, an open floor plan will encourage healthful endeavors for your kids.

So put your media devices in or very near the kitchen, and ideally buy or create a kitchen with an open floor plan. To do otherwise is to create a maze of places too complicated for you to consistently chase your chipmunks in!

SECTION II
THE RELATIONSHIP RAMIFICATIONS OF REAL ESTATE

A great wind is blowing, and that gives you either imagination or a headache.

—CATHERINE II OF RUSSIA

The Grand Palace of Catherine the Great, Moscow. The empress bought the palace in 1776, hired a remodel, and nine years into the project in 1785 had it torn down to be rebuilt, citing it too dark. Catherine the Great died before the second remodel was complete.

6

WATERFRONT OR WAR FRONT? HOW THE PROPERTY YOU BUY AFFECTS YOUR RELATIONSHIP WITH YOUR NEIGHBORS

This life is like a swimming pool.
You dive into the water, but you can't see how deep it is.

—DENNIS RODMAN

What Rodman meant when he said this is open to debate. There's no debate, however, that waterfront property is the real-estate equivalent of a front-row seat at an NBA game: there's no more coveted location. Front-row seats and waterfront property, both command the highest dollar within their markets. In both locations, the thinking goes:

"Nothing should block my view; no one should get in my way. No one has earned this position more than I have."

In the front row or on the waterfront, you are clearly in possession of a better location than your peers. Water is our very life source, where we came from, and where we all prefer to go. Our first months of life, in fact, as unborn children were in water. Something about the shimmering soft depths of the horizon's cradle calls to us all.

"No one would pass up front-row NBA seats, and no one would pass up waterfront property." The thinking goes.

But should they?

Almost half of the world's population lives within a two-hour drive of saltwater or freshwater waterfront property. It is commonly thought "the next war will be over water." As you read this, some of the prime waterfront real estate in the United States, in California, is in a drought severe enough to warrant restaurants to stop proactively serving water without request.

Water not only is a mandatory ingredient for all life, it has the aesthetic value with regard to real estate, commanding a high dollar value. Waterfront property costs well over twice as much as nonwaterfront property (116 percent more, to be exact).[1]

If a waterfront property in your neighborhood costs $1 million, a similar house behind it or across the street will cost approximately $500,000 or less. Subsequently, the taxes on waterfront property are about twice as high. US property taxes are just over 1 percent of a home's market value; the $1 million home has about $10,000 in taxes a year, the $500,000 house about $5,000 (if you were wondering, New Jersey had the highest property taxes in 2014, according to the Tax Foundation). Indeed, the single feature of real estate that home buyers pay the most to attain is for "waterfront."[2]

As a nation, our favorite restaurants are near or on the water. The most prized rooms in the best hotels have clean views of water. Our favorite walking paths and hikes follow water or terminate in a water feature. Some of our favorite daredevil athletes and big wave surfers compete on water. It only seems natural, then, that waterfront property would be the ultimate reward for decades of toil at work—that if you were given waterfront property, you would automatically defend its borders with your strongest fight.

Most people do.

Once homeowners actually buy waterfront property, their own hard-won front-row seats, they have a foe fiercer than the IRS to wage battle with—nature. Mad hurricanes on the eastern seaboard of the United States and in the southeast have extended the ocean's grip inland, dismantling large cities without remorse. Mortgage granting banks and government entities now demand flood insurance for many waterfront homes, an admission to the powerful wanton destructive forces of nature.

When waterfront homeowners stage winning battles against the water and wind, including saltwater, freshwater and riverfront, they still incur

---

1 Zillow, "What Would You Pay to Live on the Water?" 2015. http://www.zillow.com/blog/water-front-homes-analysis-159683/.

2 National Association of Realtors, "Profile of Home Buyers and Sellers," 2013. http://www.realtor.org/sites/default/files/Highlights-NAR-HBS-2013.pdf.

substantial defense budgets. Exterior treatments and fixtures on waterfront homes—paint, siding, roofing, and windows—need routine costly maintenance to sustain the war against corrosive wind and waterborne weapons of the sea. Many waterfront homes, obviously set low near the water table, have convoluted access points for vehicles; getting cement, timber, appliances, and utilities to waterfront homes can be exponentially more troublesome than getting the same items to a simple flat lot.

The waterfront castle is the single most expensive, single most time-consuming, and single most coveted material item most people could ever hope to buy. It is understandably maintained and defended.

A castle has a king, a king rules his kingdom. Unlike medieval Europe, however, waterfront kingdoms have five feet, not five-hundred mile setbacks from each other. Where wars were fought to preserve miles, waterfront wars are waged to preserve centimeters. **No type of residential real estate is more anxiously contested than waterfront real estate.** History

Warmian Bishop's Castle, Poland. It is believed Nicolaus Copernicus wrote part of his De revolutionibus orbium coelestium here. Translation: "On the Revolutions of the Heavenly Spheres," or, the idea that the planets in our solar system revolve around the sun, not vice-versa.

shows us three distinct battles are waged.

Bloodshed for Historical Markers

Ironically, American home buyers do not generally verify the real property they are actually going to own before closing on their real estate purchases.

They pay for the $450 inspection of the roof, siding, foundation, and all appliances. Often, buyers pay an additional $200 for a home movie of their sewer line—literally a fifteen-minute video tour through their sewage! (One top inspector I know of delivers the sewer DVD with a bag of microwave popcorn.) Modern buyers bring electricians, plumbers, and even interior designers inside the home they plan on purchasing for preclosing advice.

Very rarely though, maybe 1 percent of the time, do they pay for a survey—the only physical way to verify what they are actually buying. Buyers look at homes, study fence and vegetation lines that have been in place for decades, and then ask their real-estate agents:

"Where is the property line?"
The real-estate agent points at a rock and a tree and responds, *"About where that rock and that tree line up!"*
OK, now back to that movie of your sewage.
Always get a survey. Especially on waterfront property.

Waterfront owners take ownership of their real estate in one of two ways. They were either given the property or they earned it. If they were given the property, it has probably been in the family for decades, if not a century. One to five generations of family members may have lived on the property, planted trees, and erected fences, and structures. How does anyone know that they did these things on their own property?
You don't. Not without a survey.
If it were as simple as a tree over a property line, no blood would be shed. A tree under which eight generations of family hunting hounds are buried, planted by a dead relative, though, will become a historical marker—one that its current owners might actually give their lives, and at least their time, to defending.

If someone earned waterfront property—that is to say, they worked for the resources to pay for and maintain it—they are immediately at odds with someone who was given what they had to toil for. Additionally, no one can argue they don't have a right to establish their property lines, their castle, after having saved and planned for decades to buy the property.

To the family who *paid* for the waterfront property, the tree is an encroachment on and assault to their life's diligence. They worked for a clean view, and now they want it.

To the family who *inherited* the property the tree is a historical marker and family gravestone. Anyone who threatens that is understandably evil to them.

Neither family is wrong. The neighborly war that ensues quickly becomes a small-scale American Holy War. Killed pets, killed trees, egged cars and fisticuffs are not out of the question. We admonish the generational battles in the Middle East but wage decades-long chronic stress battles with our neighbors. Over trees. Trees.

To avoid a UFC fight with your potential waterfront neighbor, get a survey, before you buy, and discuss the boundary lines with all relevant parties. Do you want to own a home where your partner, children, and pets will be drawn into a daily, anxious, skirmish with good people? There is always another property to buy, one where the borders, and historical markers, need not warrant bloodshed.

SURFACE-TO-SURFACE MISSILES

The potentiality for staunch defense of the waterfront castle doesn't end at the property line. There comes a time when missiles might become preferred armory.

Again, the recurrent costs of waterfront real-estate ownership are high: taxes, flood insurance, and maintenance. However, there is no guarantee that people who inherit waterfront property can afford to pay for them. While their emotional attachment to their family waterfront estate remains high, their ability and commitment to paying for ongoing expensive maintenance may become nonexistent. A substantial number of waterfront owners cannot functionally afford to live in a waterfront home in a respectable manner. As a result, the deferred maintenance on their homes, lots, and grounds renders them war zones.

This occurs in every neighborhood, but the difference between an immaculate waterfront home and one with severely deferred maintenance is imminently more obvious and more irksome; if you buy a front-row seat at an NBA game, you're expecting not to be disturbed by your seat mate.

The tangible challenge for waterfront homeowners, in this case, arises when they try to sell (to say nothing of the emotional distress of living next to a mound of garbage). When the waterfront owner tries to sell or refinance his or her home, it becomes more difficult, if not impossible to do. New potential homeowners who have been waiting for decades to live on the water don't want to buy next to a home and yard that looks like the backside of a Walmart.

These neighbors who disregard aesthetic normalcy and fail to maintain their homes do so in a chain of events. First, they stop paying for the correct type and level of insurance. Second, they stop doing expensive maintenance. Finally, as their age increases and their available resources decrease, they actually may slip into the depravity of hoarding. In this final

Extreme deferred maintenance on a waterfront property!

stage, all maintenance is disregarded and the home seems to be breeding trash. Landscaping, abandoned vehicles, and even garbage grow from the home and creep daily toward the neighbors.

Once this third stage of depravity sets in, only a well-placed missile could solve the problem. To avoid the need for full-scale aerial forces at your neighbor's door, when you buy waterfront property, make sure the immediate neighborhood homes are not owned by, or soon to be owned by, anyone who can't pay for the ongoing maintenance of an expensive property.

The simplest formula for doing this takes little time. First, what you probably already do, look at the neighboring homes. That's not enough, though. You will own your waterfront home for one to three decades or more. You must, second, check the mortgage balances (public information) on your neighbors' parcels. If they have mortgage balances of approximately 50 percent of the values of their homes, or higher, you know they can't simply pass the property on to anyone they like; anyone who takes it over will have to have the resources to buy them out.

If you check the mortgage balances, and they are less than 50 percent of the market value of either home, it will serve you well to simply knock on their door, politely introduce yourself as their potential new neighbor, and ask them how long they plan on staying, and how they plan on leaving the property: sale or inheritance. If they plan on giving it to loved ones, there is reason to worry.

FROM THE NBA TO MLB: AN ALL AMERICAN, THE AFRICAN SAVANNAH, AND THE FIGHT FOR A CLEAN VIEW.

John Olerud was a celebrated and highly talented Major League Baseball player who built his family home in a prominent neighborhood in Bellevue, Washington. After almost two decades in the Major Leagues, including two World Series victories, he moved in with the Baker family on Clyde Hill, Bellevue, Washington, while he developed his family home behind the Bakers' house. Upon finishing the home—then worth an estimated $4 million—his family moved into it and subsequently engaged in a multiyear confrontation with the Bakers to remove two trees from their property that blocked a significant portion of his potential Seattle City and Lake Washington views.

Olerud commissioned an appraisal showing the trees devalued his home by over $250,000, and after several years of back and forth, he won a ruling from the local city council forcing the Bakers to remove the two fifty-plus-foot trees, conditional upon paying the Bakers about $63,000.

Olerud called the Bakers out for being unchristian for their stubbornness with regard to removing the trees:

"I'm just making the point that if you're willing to cut down your own trees to maintain your view and yet you aren't willing to offer that to your neighbor, how is that being a good neighbor? The Bible says, 'Love the Lord your God with all your heart, soul and strength, and your neighbor as yourself.' That's Jesus' commandment."[3]

It's unknown whether or not God wanted the trees removed.

It is known, though, according to some prominent scholars, that Olerud may have been driven by primal subconscious motives with regard to his view preference. In a book important to environmental advocates, Green Nature, Human Nature, Charles A. Lewis draws on a collection of studies and theories to conclude that human beings prefer generally open views.

Humans developed in the African Savannah, the argument goes, and needed to be able to see most of the landscape in front of them to survive and subsequently advance as a species.[4] Maybe Olerud was acting off a deep, primal desire to get a clear picture of what was in front of him. Maybe it was only natural he was inspired to enhance his view, an inborn instinct to see the world clearly in front of him.

Take whichever side you like, the Gold Glove winner's or the Bakers'. But, there is no denying human beings tend to create open views from all of our constructs. Our homes, vehicles, and seating at any important event are valued by their open views. Would you rather have a seat at the World Series partially obstructed by a pillar or one in the owner's luxury suite?

When views are at stake, people enforce and defend them fiercely. Nowhere is this more prevalent than in the front row, at the waterfront.

On waterfront property, though, unlike the Bakers' 250-foot trees, small view impediments become big deals. A single bamboo stalk. The nighttime lighting of an American flag. A power line that one neighbor refuses to pay to have buried. All of these items can, do, and will become larger fights, significant contributions to the chronic stress levels of your family. Isn't the idea of owning waterfront property is that your stress decreases?

If you are buying waterfront property, consider how protectable the

3 Keith Ervin, "Tree Fosters Dispute over What's a Good Neighbor," Seattle Times, Sep-tember 10, 2012.

4 Charles A. Lewis, Green Nature, Human Nature: The Meaning of Plants in Our Lives (First Illinois, 1996).

view is. Also, as the Olerud example here shows, consider whether your property can or will impact someone else's view. As we approach the waterfront, prices increase, as does tension and the potential to impact what other people think they are owed. It's not that these problems don't exist on streets without waterfront properties or views; this is simply something to consider when considering high-end waterfront neighborhoods. Waterfront property is expensive, financially and emotionally. Ironically, waterfront property owners tend not to buy it twice. Whether or not you plan on buying it once, it's not as serene as you might imagine.

7

"IF YOU BUILD IT, THEY WILL COME": YOUR HOME AND THE QUALITY OF THE RELATIONSHIP WITH YOUR CHILDREN

Hey, Dad? You wanna have a catch?

—**KEVIN COSTNER** AS RAY KINSELLA,
CLOSING SCENE OF *FIELD OF DREAMS*

Whap.

The sound of leather hardball snapping into an open mitt may conjure the most visceral sensory experience you recall as a child. The feel of a dirty scratched baseball lodged perfectly in your glove, your sweat mixing with sand inside the glove to create a wonderfully natural fit.

Maybe it wasn't baseball. Maybe it was football, tennis, or soccer. Really, any timeless mutual exchange of a piece of sports equipment, traded on equal terms back and forth without tangible purpose. Just playing catch. For many people, this simple game was the formative, neutral grounds to connect with their parents.

The game of playing catch is generally a noncompetitive activity. If a parent and child pretend that they are playing in an actual event, they often will imagine themselves on the same team:

It's a grounder to the shortstop (child), he flips to the second basemen (father) who then rifles it to the first baseman (child) for a double play.

One-on-one basketball, bowling, and tennis, however, generally develop into a competition. ("I finally beat you!") What difference does this make to families? What difference does it make to the flow of conversation during and after the

game? The role of talk in family sports can indeed be crucial.

There may be no more poignant parent-to-child event than the emotion passed back and forth by the simple trading of a ball. Playing catch for many parents, fathers, especially, may also be the single most practiced measurable activity a parent does to play with their child. A seemingly trivial pastime is often used to forge and reconcile in the case of Ray Kinsella (Kevin Costner), parent-to-child bonds.

Much of the evidence linking fathers to their children's social competence comes back to the way they play with their children.[1]

—PAUL RAEBURN

Fathers spend about seven hours a week caring for their children (about one-half of what mothers do), and almost one-half of fathers report they get too little time with their children (the vast majority of mothers get

---

1 Paul Raeburn, Do Fathers Matter?: What Science Is Telling Us About the Parent We've Over-looked (Scientific American/Farrar, Straus and Giroux, United States of America June 2014).

enough, or even too much, time with their kids).[1] If dads get about an hour a day to directly influence their children's growth and development, how does their home affect their relationship with their children?

Is Play Play?

Geographically, Seattle, Washington, is about as far away from anything in the United States as you can get. Despite historic and ongoing technological business, it was still a sports black hole until 2014 when the Seattle Seahawks won a Superbowl, breaking the thirty-plus year seal on professional sports prowess in the city.

Even though Seattle is the Silicon Sound of technology, its citizens uniformly, often obsessively, relate to the city's football team. Just ask Hudson, an eight-year-old who lives next door to some friends of mine, Mr. and Mrs. Campus, south of Seattle.

Mr. and Mrs. Campus have known Hudson for about five years now, and starting in 2014, when the Seahawks won the Superbowl, the dusty-blond neighbor boy, a real-life production of Calvin from *Calvin and Hobbes* has wandered regularly to their home for a fix. I remember going to my neighbor's home for candy as a kid. Hudson goes to play catch.

Mr. Campus was a division-one collegiate football player and part-time high-school football coach.; I can't imagine anyone better to play catch with. The "catch," though, turned into sixty-minute practices. Hudson started demanding a playbook, names for plays, and professional-level commitment for getting the plays right. This is not Russell Wilson; this is an eight-year-old.

The last time I saw him play with Mr. Campus, he had demanded they run every play exactly ten times, to make sure they got it right. During one set, Hudson skidded to the ground to make a catch and got up with a rose thorn in his knee. He pulled it out, laughed, and finished the set of ten. His mother had a nearly impossible task when she tried to break up the practices for Hudson's dinner.

Puzzled as to the strict regime of ten practice plays, I asked Hudson why the practice was so important:

---

1 http://www.pewsocialtrends.org/2013/03/14/modern-parenthood-roles-of-moms-and-dads-converge-as-they-balance-work-and-family/.

"We play football every day at recess, all year long. I have to be good at it so I can fit in."

There is no understating the import of "play" in the life of any developing human being. Hudson clearly understands and can verbally express the importance of play as a social bonding agent both with his peers and also with a positive male adult. But play, in its many forms, is proven to have vital developmental impacts on children as shown below:

—Increased executive function—the ability of a child to self-regulate their behavior (think of Hudson demanding sets of ten plays)
—Improved literacy
—Improved learning
—The forging of positive child to adult interaction
—Improved cognitive ability
—Improved social skills
—Improved physical health

Specifically, positive and ample interaction between a father and child is likely to lead to higher IQ for the child, fewer behavioral problems, less depression for daughters, and even lower rates of smoking.

Children spend their leisure time doing three main types of activities. "Free play," the variations of which Hudson practiced in the example above; structured play, or actually going to flag-football practice; and finally passive activity, like watching television or playing video games.

No case can be made that all three types of activities are not fundamental and positive in the correct doses. Even the most stubborn of pure-minded mothers can admit it is important for modern children to use and adapt to electronic devices and media. A child raised without any exposure to electronic media would be a modern-day version of Tarzan, raised in the wild and short on public etiquette.

Also as obvious, electronic media consumption as the only leisure activity for a child would lead to an adult who might struggle in the "jungle" of the working world. Down and dirty, fresh aired, rough and tumble uncontrolled play is simply the way children learn successful tactics for interaction in and with the world.

Buying a (Play) House

How does your home choice affect your child's level of play?

If you acknowledge that free play, for example, imaginary football practice, is important to your children's development, only you can create the backdrop and the venue for the activity. Further, if you want your share of childcare time, again about seven hours per week for fathers and about fourteen hours per week for mothers, to include free play, you must, first, choose a home in a neighborhood with a high degree of perceived safety.

Not necessarily actual safety but perceived safety.

In the home you currently reside in, or the one you are considering buying or renting, can you imagine letting your eight-year-old play catch or shoot hoops unsupervised in the front yard? For most people, there is an immediate and clear answer to this question. The factors that contribute to the answer, though, are several.

Let's go back to Hudson, in Seattle, and the basketball setup in his front yard. Lacking an NBA team in Seattle, Hudson wears a red Washington Wizards John Wall jersey when he plays imaginary NBA playoff games. When he misses a shot, gravity takes it back toward his home, away from the street. Additionally, the street that he lives on has a speed limit of twenty-five miles per hour. More importantly, about seventy-five feet from his backboard, the street takes a sharp turn that forces drivers to slow down in front of his house.

This is a good street and a good front yard to encourage individual or group free play. It makes going to, waiting in, and playing in the yard and surroundings safe.

The Campuses are retired, home most days, and actively in and out of their driveway all day. Their other neighbors, neighbors to Hudson as well, have two young girls, the mother of whom is home most days. Adjacent Hudson's home on the other side are neighbors, a vigilant and immaculately clean married couple. It is not, however, a high-end or new-construction neighborhood. Generally, their neighborhood is humble and understated.

Hudson's neighbors all have nearly unimpeded views of Hudson's basketball court and monitor his safety, as does Hudson's mom from her kitchen. All parents have deep fears about child abduction, strangers, and any ill-intended visitors to their neighborhood. But Hudson's basketball court is almost never without eyes on it; its perceived safety level is high.

The basketball court is a natural and safe place for him to go.

What children are allowed to do with their free time, and with whom, is less a conscious decision by any parent and more a function of the cost-benefit analysis of their activity and its second-best alternative. This is to say, because Hudson's mom *feels* safe about his basketball court and because his friends' mothers do as well, his mom can tell him to turn the television off and get outside. Inevitably, other people, including his friends and mentors, meet him there for games of PIG.

The opposite is true if there is latent fear for Hudson's safety while shooting hoops. His mom may know, and want, free play and physical activity to occur, but at what cost? If she is worried about her son disappearing or chasing a ball into busy traffic, television is a better option. This is true for many family units. Parents don't proactively decide watching television is their preferred pastime for their child; they simply default to it because of its perceived safety.

While Hudson's basketball venue is rich in home-field safety, his home is not ostensibly modern or fancy. Despite his mother's acute sense of style, profession as a corporate executive, and resources, she picked an older home in an older neighborhood without a modern master suite or open-concept floor plan. Hudson's mom chose Field of Dreams, and now her son has daily unimpeded access to shooting hoops.

KIDDY WALKABILITY

Back to playing catch:

If you have to put your child in a car to physically recreate, the odds you will do so together are less likely. Consider Hudson. At home, he can shoot hoops for five minutes or fifty minutes. Any neighbor, and his mom, can move casually in and out of his game while attending to other household chores and duties. If at any point in time Hudson tires of basketball, he can move onto football or invent another childhood game alone, with his mom, or with friends.

If Hudson's yard offered no functional space for these activities, and functional space was not nearby, his mom would have to put him into a car to take him to play. Because taking him somewhere is a larger commitment of energy, his mom would want a higher physical payback for him, more than forty-five minutes, from whatever form of play he was to engage in. Naturally, without nearby space to practice free play, structured play becomes the unintended sole option for activity: sports teams.

Again, structured play, like playing on a flag-football team, is very important for children. But, it lacks development of imagination, executive direction, and social self-governance. Children need these for their highest levels of personal satisfaction and achievement.

Your yard does not have to be big enough for neighborhood games of "kick the can" to mandate safe free play for your child. Additional venues—parks, green spaces, personal sport courts, and safe cul-de-sacs—could be available within a single Tiger Woods drive off the tee. Further than that, and the average child in the average neighborhood has to cross too many intersections on the walk to the neighborhood park.

Again, the perceived safety of the walk to the local park decreases with distance until the cost of allowing the child to go there increases sufficiently to outweigh all the physical, social, and developmental benefits of being allowed to go there. Without adequate, safe, local play space, television rightly becomes the childhood leisure that makes sense.

Every home for every buyer or renter at every price level is a function of trade-offs. No buyer, no matter their wealth, ever has a perfect home. If they did, they would never sell their homes or buy additional ones. Within your budget, among the trade-offs you are forced to choose, are decisions that lead to more play and less play. How important is it to you to play catch with your child? When you choose your next home, to a large degree, you will dictate how often you and your family members will engage in healthy, relationship forging free play.

8

DOES THE TIMING OF YOUR HOME PURCHASE AFFECT THE QUALITY OF YOUR ROMANTIC RELATIONSHIP?

The average wedding costs about $30,000.[1] The most common down payment for first-time home buyers, based on the median price of an American home,[2] is about $6,244. About one-half of first-time home buyers use an FHA 3.5 percent down payment loan.

If you reverse these statistics, your first marriage is much more likely to be happy—you should be spending about $30,000 cash on your first down payment and far less on your wedding. Generally speaking, the more you spend on a wedding, the more likely it is to end in divorce.[3] Make sure to invite lots of friends, though, and to go on a honeymoon, because those factors are associated with likelihood of a more successful marriage!

What about testing a relationship before marriage? What about the pre-commitment move-in? Most people have considered moving in with their

---

1 Sarah Portlock. Wall Street Journal, Online Edition. October 24, 2014. http://blogs.wsj.com/economics/2014/10/24/will-a-cheap-wedding-help-your-marriage-a-lesson-in-causation/.

2 Zillow. http://www.zillow.com/home-values/.

3 See note 28.

partner to "test" the relationship. When is the right time to do this?

Multiple studies have shown cohabitation, living with someone before getting married or engaged to them, is associated with the following:

—lower marital satisfaction
—lower interpersonal commitment from men
—poorer communication during marriage
—more marital conflict
—higher rates of female spousal infidelity
—higher likelihood of divorce[4]

The association of higher divorce rates of people who cohabitated before advancing their relationship has been shown to exist in multiple studies.[5] The cause, though, is unclear: Are only certain types of "not marriage-type" people cohabitating and then subsequently getting married? Or does living together before marriage cause higher divorce rates?

In either case, the strong emotional and financial pulls to "test out" a relationship are generally not associated with positive results: happier, longer marriages. You've been there—living out of a gym bag and rotating bedrooms to have time with someone you are in love with gets old fast. Buying the second toothbrush is cheap, whereas acquiring or maintaining another home that you won't need, whether a rental or purchase, is not.

Scholars explain relationship inertia that may lead people deep into interpersonal quicksand when they preemptively move in together. First, the couple without a committed relationship rents or buys a new home. They abandon ties to their old home, community, and, to some degree, friends. Next, the couple buys home furnishings together. They begin commingling utility accounts. The couple gets used to new daily paths, habits, and locations. As the events occur, over zero to ninety days, the functional commitment of the relationship grows.

Every step taken means any step or steps backward become harder. The problem is that the basis of the relationship—the fundamental com-

---

4 Galena H. Kline et al., "Timing is Everything: Pre-Engagement Cohabitation and Increased Risk for Poor Marital Outcomes," Journal of Family Psychology 18, no. 2 (2004): 311–18.

5 Many studies have shown an association with cohabitation and inferior relationships. Recently, some studies have shown this association lessening and, in one case, disappearing, apparently due to the increased occurrence of cohabitation before commitment in a relationship. More studies can and will clarify the association, but due to the constantly changing nature of shifting modern relationship practices, a perfect association of result and explanation is not available.

munication, connection, and romantic attributes—may be decreasing while functional commitment increases. Very easily, the couple finds themselves functionally bound together without the emotional component of the relationship having grown, developed, and increased. At the end of three, six, twelve, or more months, it may simply seem much easier to get married than to find a new place to live, buy new furniture, and set up another home.

Relationship inertia pulls the couple forward until they may be stuck without help, chest-deep in emotional quicksand. Before they know it, the couple may be married without ever having established crucial communication and problem solving skills.

COLD, DEEP WATER

Where relationship inertia can pull a bad relationship into a deeper, more committed pond, it can also pull a good one preemptively into deep water too quickly. People who have known each other for a short amount of time have not developed the communication (fighting) skills they need to interact. In the first six to twelve months of most relationships, romance is high and arguments low or nonexistent.

During this time, if there are arguments, they are over smaller topics and with less emotion. As the relationship develops, larger and more serious topics are brought to the table for discussion. If a couple has developed and refined their communication dynamic over "small" topics, it is an easier natural progression toward "large" topics. If a couple moves in together too soon, they are forced to tackle many small arguments and large ones at the same time and without much practice.

This is analogous to a novice runner committing to a marathon in a year's time and running twenty-six miles the first day of training. The novice simply isn't ready. He or she will be in six to nine months, but there exists a standard healthy escalation to running distances and intensity, and this process is vital to success. Running too far and too hard too soon leads to injury.

This is not to say moving in with a significant other after three, six, or nine months is doomed to fail. Many couples have proven this is not the case. It does mean, however, that you may run a potentially great relationship into the ground too hard and too fast. Here's what you can expect to feel if you move in with someone very quickly or without a formal commitment:

—Loss of personal freedoms: space, time, and friends
—Feelings of entrapment: "What have I done?"
—Preemptive diagnosis that the relationship is bad when in fact you would have just created a situation that made it bad
—Confusion: "I thought I finally met someone who understood me!"
—Inequity: both parties feel like they are giving more than the other

All of these, of course, are normal feelings in the course of most relationships in one form or another. Taken together, after just meeting each other, they could present one large sign that the relationship is bad and not meant to be. This is a shame if all the relationship needed was more time in a more manageable interpersonal stage. It may have just needed some jogging before an all-out attempt at a marathon!

CASE-SHILLER AND THE MATHEMATICAL EXPLANATION FOR THE SEVEN-YEAR ITCH

The average divorcing American does so after eight years of marriage. Coincidentally, using the Case-Shiller index over the last thirty years, the average American has "broken even" on their home purchase after about eight years.

Over the last thirty years, nationwide, according to the most frequently used measure of the United States' real-estate market, real-estate appreciation has averaged approximately 1.3 percent per year. Consider the following:

• The average American home is worth about $178,400 at the time of printing this book according to the Zillow Home Price Index.
• Using 1.3 percent appreciation, from data gathered over the last thirty years (in seven years), a home bought today would be worth $195,281.
• Using 8.5 percent as a baseline amount for the closing costs

associated with selling a home, the seller of this home will have seen enough appreciation to make $282 above and beyond their initial purchase price.[6]

Hmmm.

The average American homeowner sees proceeds above their initial purchase price in seven years.

If a couple is going to get divorced, it typically happens in the eighth year (or about one year after they start to realize profit above and beyond their initial purchase price).

What comes first? The chicken, the egg, or the hen house? When, where, and how Americans decide to live affects when, where, and how their partner relationship will occur. While the numbers and studies are complex, the reality of successful mature partnership is not: make a firm decision on your relationship before you make a firm decision on your home, rental or purchase, because once you buy a home, you will be there for a while!

Specifically, your decision to cohabitate, particularly when buying a home, can affect how long you will stay in a poor relationship or, conversely, how good a relationship can be. If it takes seven years to realize profit above and beyond your purchase price of your house, you are dollars—and sense—ahead to postpone cohabitation until your relationship is firm. This is a real-estate agent telling you to put off buying; buy a second toothbrush before you buy a home together.

6 Author's note—The Zillow Home Value Index is the chosen measure of true current home pricing for the purposes of this book. The Case-Schiller Index, however, has been used far longer than the Zillow Home Value Index and is obviously the institutionally accepted measure of home price appreciation over a far greater span of time than the Zillow Home Value Index. Subsequently, when real-estate values over large spans of time are needed for example in this book, Case-Shiller is used. But when giving modern examples of home prices, Zillow is used. Both methods are professional and reliable, if not totally agreeable; this is not an attempt to market or promote one over the other.

9

HOW DO YOUR NEIGHBORS AFFECT YOUR DIET, YOUR RELATIONSHIP STATUS, YOUR SPENDING HABITS, AND HOW OFTEN YOU RIDE YOUR BIKE?

"So they keep to themselves, can you blame them? They live next door to people who break in their house, and burn it down while they're gone for the day!"

—TOM HANKS
AS RAY PETERSON IN *THE 'BURBS*

The 'Burbs, perhaps the best Tom Hanks comedy made, perfectly suggests the way you should behave in your neighborhood—the same as your neighbors. If you don't, you will be socially pushed to the outside of your local community.

"I'm telling you these people are Satanists. As I sit here, they are satanists. Look, look, the world is full of these kind of things—black masses, mutilations. Mutilations! The incubus, the succubus—I'm tellin' you, Walter [an elderly neighbor who is missing] was a human sacrifice."

—RICK DUCOMMON
AS ART, TOM HANKS'S NEIGHBOR IN *THE 'BURBS*

Hanks and Ducommon recognize obvious differences with their neighbors in the movie, the set of which is still partially erected and was used for *Desperate Housewives* in Universal Studios, Hollywood. Because their neighbors act askew, they theorize the neighbors are operating some sort of sick crematorium in their basement.

If you act, dress, decorate, and recreate differently than your neighbors, you may not fit in. We're not only talking about the condition of your garden beds and vitality of your grass. The psychological need to mirror your neighbors' behavior extends to important categories of your life.

No matter who your best friends *were*, where you *are* dictates who your friends will be now. Friendship is defined by shared experience. To a large degree, your neighbors become your active influencers.

For example, think about those people you are closest to right now—not the people you were closest to or want to be close to, but those people whom you are close to. The majority of these people are very likely people with whom you share weekly, if not daily, interaction with. This could mean working out at the same time, eating lunch together, coaching a children's sport team together, or working with them on a fund raiser.

We tend to emotionally catalog our best friends as if the friendships were proactive choices. They really are not. They are a direct function of shared routine task together. Think about who your friends were in college or the military. You met them at your dorm, in your classes, or during your sport. You shared one commonality with them, saw them routinely, and developed a bond. Their other skills, traits, and habits were not important. In college, you did not pick your friends from a catalog; you simply bumped into them continuously doing the same things.

These are friendships.

This is important because the neighborhood you buy in can influence who your friends are. This one common trait, location, can dictate your friendship. The other values and practices of these friends may or may not be in line with yours. Neighborhood, here, means any social or geographic community: a condo building, a cul-de-sac, or a classic suburban street. It includes social, religious, and political communities.

It is well documented that growing up in a crime-ridden neighborhood makes it much more likely that individuals who grew up there will participate in crime during the course of their life. The same is true of obesity: obesity as a neighborhood demographic trait is more likely to produce obese individuals. Both of these trends, however, are acutely linked to poverty and poorer neighborhoods. What about other neighborhoods, like your neighborhood?

—If your neighbor uses a bicycle for transportation, it is more likely you will too.[1]

—If you grew up in the top 20 percent of neighborhoods, you will make $901,000 more in your lifetime.[2]

—If your neighbors are happily married, it is likely they will help model your relationship that way.[3]

—If your neighbors get divorced, it is more likely you will too.[4]

—If your neighbor buys a new car, it's a strong sign you soon will be as well.[5]

What happens to your committed relationship if you move into a community of single, transitory people in a condo building? People do this all the time. The people around you are dating, dining, and mingling. How would this affect your perception of your own relationship?

What happens if you move into a neighborhood of stay-at-home mothers, but you are a mother who works outside the home? Will you be accepted in this neighborhood? How will you feel about going to work when these women don't? How will you feel playing with your own children in your own front yard after work, when the other mothers are coming out to chat after a day at home?

There is no good that comes from judging any of these lifestyles. Your own welfare, however, is dictated by living out your own values. It would behoove you, before moving to a certain neighborhood, to knock on about five doors and introduce yourself, take a walk in the neighborhood, and spend one hour in a the local park with your pets and loved ones. Do these people that you meet promote and inspire your values, or would they tempt the opposites?

1 Chih-Hao Wanga, Gulsah Akarb, and Jean-Michel Guldmann, "Do Your Neighbors Affect Your Bicycling Choice? A Spatial Probit Model for Bicycling to The Ohio State University," Journal of Transport Geography (2015). http://www.researchgate.net/publication/271019677_Do_Your_Neighbors_Affect_Your_Bicy-cling_Choice_A_Spatial_Probit_Model_for_Bicycling_to_the_Ohio_State_University.

2 Jonathan T. Rothwell and Douglas S. Massey, "Geographic Effects on Intergenerational Income Mobility," Economic Geography (January 2015). http://onlinelibrary.wiley.com/doi/10.1111/ecge.12072/abstract.

3 Rose McDermott, James Fowler, and Nicholas Christakis, "Breaking Up is Hard to Do, Unless Everyone Else is Doing it Too: Social Network Effects on Divorce in a Longitudinal Sample," Published in final edited form as: Social Forces 92, no. 2 (December 2013): 491–519. , 2014http://www.ncbi.nlm.nih.gov/pmc/articles/PMC3990282/.

4 Ibid.

5 Mark Grinblatt, Matti Keloharju, and Seppo Ikäheimo, "Interpersonal Effects in Consumption: Evidence from the Automobile Purchases of Neighbors," September 30, 2003. http://www.haas.berkeley.edu/groups/finance/Berkeley%20paper.pdf.

Look at who lives in the neighborhood you are considering and ask, "Do I want to become that?"

WHICH IS THE BIGGER DISCOUNT— BUYING A FORECLOSURE OR BUYING NEXT TO A SEX OFFENDER?

Research indicates the foreclosure discount, the discount you would receive for buying a foreclosed home, is at its lowest rate in at least a decade: 7.7 percent.[6] That is to say, you could buy a foreclosed home for $200,000 that would have cost about $215,000 sold in the open market.

You will receive a greater discount if you buy a home next to a sex offender, and he or she subsequently moves: 12 percent.[7] Homes directly adjacent to sex offenders suffer a 12 percent price drop that immediately corrects itself when the offender moves. That is to say, if you bought a home next to an offender for $200,000, it could immediately increase in price to $224,000 when they moved out.

While these statistics are interesting, they are emotionally unattractive. There is no question, though, that your neighbors can and do have a large effect on your life, particularly the value of your home and the quality of your life.

WHAT YOU CALL HOARDING, AN APPRAISER CALLS EXTERNAL OBSOLESCENCE

External obsolescence is an appraisal-industry term that refers to factors outside of a homeowner's control that decrease the market value of the home. Consider living next to a junky yard, utility towers, or a train track external obsolescence. Unfortunately, your neighbors can create physical features that devalue your home.

If you live next to the Klopeks from the movie *The 'Burbs*, your home

6 Spencer Rascoff and Stan Humpheries., Zillow Talk. (Grand Central Publishing, New York, 2015), 89.

7 Leigh Linden and Jonah E. Rockoff, "Estimates of the Impact of Crime Risk on Property Values from Megan's Laws," American Economic Review 98, no. 3 (2008): 1103–27. http://www.leighlinden.com/Megans_Law_AER.pdf.

has external obsolescence, probably in the range of 0–10 percent. This is to say, living next to this family can and does cost you money with respect to the sale price of your home. As you have learned, though, your sales price is not the only effect your neighbor's lifestyle has on yours.

10

WHICH GRANDPARENTS SHOULD YOU LIVE NEAR FOR THE BENEFIT OF THE FAMILY?

With childcare in the United States costing up to nearly $1,400 a month per child in expensive American states,[1] it's no surprise that most Americans live within approximately twenty-five miles of their parents.[2] Which set of parents should you live close to? The answer has a surprising effect on your family dynamics: an approximate 40 percent swing in the likelihood or unlikelihood of divorce depending on which set of the parents you develop strong bonds with.[3]

In 2014, infant childcare cost Americans from $546 per month to $1,379 per month, per child.[4] In general, child care is more expensive in the United States as you head north: Alabama and Mississippi have some of the lowest healthcare costs, Connecticut and Maryland some of the

1 Child Care Aware of America, "Child Care in America: 2014 State Fact Sheets." http://usa.childcare-aware.org/advocacy/reports-research/child-care-in-america-2014-fact-sheets/.

2 Janice Compton and Robert Pollack, "Proximity and Coresidence of Adult Children and their Parents: Description and Correlates," Michigan Retirement Research Center, October 2009.

3 Terri Orbuch, "Early Years of Marriage Project," Institute for Social Research, University of Michigan.

4 See note 41.

highest:

> Checkout "Reports and Research" at www.usa.childcareaware.
> org. The 2014 data here is highly interesting, very detailed, very spe-
> cific, and still easily readable.

For married couples, this was approximately 7–19 percent of their income. (Single women have to use 26–65 percent of their income for childcare!) Childcare can easily be the biggest cost, excluding rent, for American families.

Childcare will probably cost you more than college tuition at an in-state school. Midrange childcare costs $8,000 to over $11,000 per year, depending on what type of child care it is.[5] The average cost of in-state college tuition in America is $9,139 per year.[6] Additionally, depending on the number of children you have, childcare costs can creep depressingly close to your monthly housing rent.

It's no surprise that mothers and grandmothers provide the best and most affordable care for their kin. Mothers are more likely than fathers to take care of elderly family members. Grandmothers are more likely than grandfathers to provide childcare. The grandmother you develop a strong bond with can have a large impact on the happiness of your own marriage. Which grandmother should you strategically live closer to?

MEET THE FOCKERS

The scary truth about the wife to mother-in-law relationship is that it can be inherently competitive:

> *"Mothers- and daughters-in-law are supposed to be family, yet they don't know each other well. What to call each other? How much to share? There is no script. The uncertainty itself can lead to jealousy, anger, or sadness. The more uncertainty there is, the more each woman is likely to keep the other at arm's length. This can destabilize the marriage: When his mother and his wife are battling, a man's self-*

5 Ibid.

6 The College Board, Annual Survey of Colleges. 2014–2015 Data. http://trends.collegeboard.org/college-pricing/figures-tables/2014-15-in-state-tuition-fees-public-four-year-state-five-year-percentage-change.

preservation instinct tells him to hide."

—ELIZABETH BERNSTEIN[7]

Out of financial necessity, many families naturally look to their tribal elders, their grandmothers and great grandmothers, for childcare. On paper, it seems a perfect plan:

—Save about $1,000 per month, per child, on daycare costs.
—Instigate mandated social interaction with important relatives; if Grandma is the babysitter, the grandchildren and other family members get to see her regularly—and she gets to see them!
—Put your child or children in the care of someone you know intimately. They are almost guaranteed safety.

These are all tangible, undeniable, positive benefits of in-family daycare. The free babysitting, though, is not so free. The grandmother's service, babysitting, comes with a price:

—Grandma tends to feel entitled to be more critical about the rearing of the grandchildren. Importantly, she is more critical of her son's wife than of her daughter's husband.
—Grandma and Grandpa feel more comfortable, and again entitled, to stop by their children's home without notice.
—Grandma's natural feelings of inherent worry for her son ("Is he being cared for properly? Will he visit me less often?").

These combine to stoke a naturally embedded competition between a woman and her daughter-in-law that does not exist between a mother and her own daughter. This leads to frustration and retreat for both sexes and a higher likelihood of divorce—20 percent more. Divorce is about 20 percent less likely if the husband forms a strong bond with his wife's parents.[8]

While family-provided childcare can be undeniably beneficial, it is important the mother-in-law relationship be managed. Home location,

7 ELIZABETH BERNSTEIN, The Wall Street Journal Online Edition, May 2013 - http://www.wsj.com/articles/SB10001424127887324787004578495062128171822

8 Terri Orbuch, "Early Years of Marriage Project," Institute for Social Research, University of Michigan.

with respect to your in-laws, is the best way to do this. Before you buy a home that places you near one of the grandmothers, consider the natural relationship dynamic that it will create.

Grandma can always babysit, but how close to her do you need to be? While statistics tell us most Americans will stay within twenty-five miles anyway, it may be harmful to your marriage to move so close that grandma doesn't have to consider the commute before she comes over. There isn't a perfect number of miles for this equation, but if it's easier for Grandma to go to your home than to Starbucks, guess where she's getting her coffee!

If you have to move close to a grandmother for childcare, it's more likely to benefit the family as a whole if you place the mother in your home near her own mom. This seems to be create teamwork. Moving the mother in your home close to the father's mom could set up a competition.

To a significant degree, where Mom and Dad choose to live creates the weather and the backdrop that will impact their own relationship. Living nearer Mom's mom dictates sunny skies and smoother sailing. Living nearer Dad's mom dictates rougher water.

Either case can obviously work. But if you decide to move close to Dad's mom, the father in the household needs to go out of his way to express primary allegiance to his wife, as opposed to his mother. As many families have proven, if he is clear to his mother who his primary allegiance and bond is with now—his wife—he can head off any potential Superbowl-level competition of mothering skills.

If he is to put his wife nearer his own mom, he needs to know that the boundary lines must be drawn: when Grandma can stop over, how long she could stay, and what she is entitled to do as far as parenting. These are all challenging things for a son to tell his mom, so putting a little geographical distance in between himself and his mother may be easier.

How close will mom be to her mother-in-law? This may be the only case where you can consider a bad commute a good thing—putting a healthy distance between them for a good relationship.

Many home buyers shop for homes with a guest room for family members and friends to stay in when they come to town. Just remember—if you make it too nice, they may not leave!

It's your house, not a hotel. It's also likely you have guests who overstay and unlikely that you enjoy this.

There is inherent strain in hosting and entertaining guests. It is fun, meaningful, and mandatory, but it's also time consuming when the social interaction, food preparation, and cleaning are considered. There is definitely a "right" amount of time for relatives to stay.

If you make their stay too comfortable, their stays will get longer and longer. In some cases, they become a near-permanent resident, or weekly guest, at a home.

Your guest space should be comfortable and functional but not lavish and hospitable to the point of never-ending stays. Once you buy this space, it's very hard to turn people down to use it. As a general rule, if you make a nicer living situation then they have at home, you may run into trouble. Why would they ever stay home if they have a free, nicer, hotel at your home?

11

COHABITATING WITH... COWORKERS?

A t the end of a workday, how do you feel if you bump into a co-worker while waiting in line at the grocery store?

Is this something you don't mind, or even look forward to? Or, is this something you dread?

If you don't mind bumping into a coworker, your boss, or an employee after your workday is through, it is very likely you are extroverted. Extroverted people are energized by social interaction.

If the thought of bumping into a coworker in the grocery store line at the end of your workday exhausts you, you are probably introverted. Introverted people are de-energized by social interaction. The more interaction, the worse for an introvert.

It's not that introverts don't like people or that they can't be successful with other people; it's simply that they need time alone throughout the course of the day to reenergize. This could be a walk alone, having coffee alone, reading in a quiet, controlled room, or simply watching television alone for twenty minutes. Introverted people need space like they need oxygen, (just on a more frequent basis). They have to have some space to operate at their full capacity.

If introverts do not get space, they get tired, cranky, and brooding. I know because I am one.

Getting Close with Coworkers

It's not easy to say whether or not you should make friends with your coworkers at work.

—Fifty percent of people who claim to have a good friend at work report a high affinity for and satisfaction with their company. Only 10 percent of people without a good friend at work report the same thing.[1]
—Being better friends with your coworkers in general leads to
   • better communication;
   • a more fun work environment;
   • higher productivity; and
   • greater creativity.
—Real friends, as opposed to those used for social prowess, work better in teams at work.

However,

—a strong friendship at work can lead other workers to feel like you are favored, creating jealousy;
—friendships at work can potentially create a divisive work environment, as opposed to a cohesive one;
—workplace friendships generally create more, not less, stress;
—delivery of criticism, and the way it is received, is harder to do with people who are friends as well as coworkers.

So there's not an immediately obvious universal answer to the question "Should I become friends with my coworkers?"

But what about making friends with coworkers outside of work: at home, in your community, and in your personal social spheres? There is a

1 Gallup, 2012. http://www.gallup.com/services/178514/state-american-workplace.aspx.

clear answer here, and it depends upon your own personality.

Approximately one-half of your waking hours will be spent at your job and/or commuting to it. The other half of your life—eating, working out, recreating, and socializing—has sweeping effects on your work life, particularly your positive outlook on your job and work environment.

If you live in the same neighborhood as your boss, chances are you shop at the same stores. You also probably have children about the same age, who do some of the same things and may be on some of the same teams. Both of your spouses probably know each other and know people who know of each other. If you live and work in the same neighborhood, your social life and your work life are importantly connected.

If you are extroverted, this may not bother you. These additional, nonrequired interactions with your boss may be perceived as opportunities to bond and subsequently advance in the work place. If your wives are exchanging recipes at the local little league games, this may give you a great sense of comfort, a feeling that your employment and workplace opportunities are maximized.

If you are introverted, seeing your boss at yoga after work might send shivers down your spine. Yoga may be your place to relax, *your* space. That yoga class is your chance to reenergize. As an introvert, if you don't get your personal space in a given day, it will run you ragged.

Your job obviously draws on a finite collection of energy you have in any given day. The more energy you use at work, the less you have for your close relationships, your health, and your hobbies. The energy that work requires is multiplied for introverted people in the common workplace. Most modern work environments are inadvertently structured in favor of extroverted people.

As an introvert, if your job is commanding the lion's share of your daily energy, you would be wise to guard your "free" time closely. If this free time becomes more social time, especially with your coworkers, you might be setting yourself up for an exhausting life.

If you are extroverted, you probably don't mind seeing your coworkers at the gym in the morning, going out to lunch with them, and meeting them for drinks after work. You probably don't care if you run into your coworkers at your child's baseball game. It is highly likely you like running into friendly coworkers at the grocery store.

If you are introverted, and you move to a community where your coworkers live, shop, walk, work out, go to church, participate in sports, and do business, all of these opportunities would present a small subconscious amount of dread. The smaller the community is, the more the chronic stress.

What if your boss's spouse coaches the local baseball team and needs players? It is pretty likely that your son will play baseball!

What if the nurse you work with is single and dating one of your friends?

What if an attorney you regularly see in court sits on the community development board and you are trying to pull off a major remodel?

None of these things in themselves is bad. Socially speaking, they may be very beneficial. But, if you are introverted, what is the emotional cost of these interactions? Does it leave you feeling trapped, like you can never escape work?

Before you buy a home, consider its social proximity to your coworkers, particularly if you are introverted. Where do your coworkers live? Is that community tight, like the houses on the quiet cul-de-sac in *The 'Burbs*? Or, is there less interaction, in which case, it might not matter to live near your coworkers.

Where will you be shopping? Who will you run into? Will your church group mirror your office tribe?

> *"Remember what you were saying about people in the burbs, Art, people like Skip, people who mow their lawn for the 800th time, and then snap? Well, that's us. It's not them, that's us. We're the ones who are vaulting over the fences, and peeking in through people's windows. We're the ones who are throwing garbage in the street, and lighting fires. We're the ones who are acting suspicious and paranoid, Art. We're the lunatics. Us. It's not them. It's us."*
>
> —HANKS, THE 'BURBS

You may need a little space from your neighbors and your coworkers.

SECTION III
THE FINANCIAL
SCIENCE OF SQUARE
FOOTAGE

I don't believe in a law to prevent a man from getting rich; it would do more harm than good. So while we do not propose any war upon capital, we do wish to allow the humblest man an equal chance to get rich with everybody else.

—**ABRAHAM LINCOLN**

The one and only house Abraham Lincoln ever owned. Springfield, Illinois.

12

WHAT IS THE TRUE FINANCIAL COST OF OWNING ONE SQUARE FOOT OF HOUSING?

A s a child, the total tradable value of any given sack lunch I had was almost negative; I could rarely find anyone to trade me a Capri Sun for a bag of broccoli. In grade school, I was the kid who had little bags of carrots, sprouts, and green peppers in my lunch bag every day. The only time my lunches had any trade value was when someone decided they wanted to play a practical joke on another kid. Then, any bag of chopped vegetables I had was in demand.

My five-foot-four, 115-pound mom, to whom I am grateful for habitualizing healthy food decisions on me, is somewhat of a hippie. You can still go to her home on any given June night and eat fresh salad with your dinner, the ingredients of which she grew in her yard.

Grandpa Herb, a jovial round giant from Chicago, Illinois, shared my mother's laughing spirit, but not her diet preference. When he came to town, he carried several extra pairs of bulging socks in his luggage. They were cover for a treasure trove of assorted chocolates that he would share with me behind closed doors and out of sight from my mom and grandma. I remember several summer nights sitting near my grandpa eating endless amounts of chocolate.

Many times his chocolates were actually rejects from a Fannie May factory; chocolates that had been misfilled or misformed. Grandpa Herb was a Depression-era spendthrift, who made a living as a salesperson of cardboard boxes throughout the city of Chicago, Illinois. He knew the exact and fastest routes to almost anywhere in a large city, and he knew the exact cost of his business. As much as the chocolate stashes, I remember another number. His cost of driving one mile:

Eight cents.

This was not the cost of only a car. This was his cost for a car, gas, insurance, and maintenance. To him, this was the real cost of owning and using a car. He analyzed the value of his sales calls using this number.

Eight cents per mile.

What is the true cost of owning a home?

The Smiths of Green Gables
Send You
Their Holiday Greetings

My father's childhood home. Evanston, Illinois

The cost of owning one square foot of real estate is about thirty-two cents per month. This is in addition to your mortgage and tax payments.

It costs thirty-two cents per month to provide utilities for, and maintain, one square foot of American housing. This is a best estimate using US Census Bureau information associated with homes in the United States.

So, if you have a bedroom in your house that you are not using, it is costing you about $46 per month, or $552 per year above and beyond your mortgage and taxes to keep that room (this would be a twelve-by-twelve-foot room or 144 total square feet). If you have a suite above your garage for guests, it is costing you about $97 per month, or $1,164/year to keep warm, dry, and maintained (this would be just over a fifteen-by-fifteen-foot room or just over three hundred total square feet).

Here is a breakdown of the contributing costs to the thirty-two cents per square foot per month:

Electricity (light)—6 cents/ft./month
Gas (heat)—3 cents
Insurance—4 cents
Water—3 cents
Trash—1 cent
Maintenance (roofing, siding, landscaping)—15 cents
Total—32 cents[1]

If you don't believe me, take out a calculator and play with the numbers based on your own home. When you figure the maintenance cost, the biggest component of the thirty-two cents, don't forget to factor in large ticket items you buy in multiyear cycles: roofs, paint, heating, and electrical systems.

These are the costs per month of one square foot of housing. The total, 32 cents per month, does not contribute to debt service—it is paid to the government, utility companies, subcontractors, or home improvement stores. It will not, strictly speaking, be "recovered." Further, thirty-two cents per month includes no cosmetic home improvement projects; the maintenance figure is not reflective of style upgrades to your home like granite surfaces, upgraded window coverings, or new millwork.

It costs you 58 percent of your mortgage payment, above and beyond the mortgage payment, to maintain your home—This is to say if your mortgage payment, not including taxes and insurance, is $2,000, you have $1,160 in monthly expenses that are not earning equity or paying debt service. This is the real cost of owning primary-residence real estate—your mortgage and tax payment plus thirty-two cents, per foot, per month.

---

1 All figures here taken from the 2015 Consumer Expenditures Survey (CE) published by the Bureau of Labor Statistics.

These costs are unavoidable if your true goal is to fully realize your profit on your real-estate asset when you sell it. You can't just turn off all the lights and let your yard go Jumanji. If you do not keep your home warm, dry, protected, and maintained, over time, the effects of deferred maintenance will alter your ability to make the long-term large profit on real estate you are expecting to make.

HIDING CHOCOLATE, HIDING TRUE COSTS

This thirty-two cents is the unspoken love child of buying a house; it exists and will make itself known. Real-estate agents and lenders don't market this figure to you when you are buying a home. But it's not a "soft" cost; it's not something you can avoid if you want to participate in true real-estate investment. The thirty-two cents per month is a fixed cost of owning an extra square foot of real estate, and it needs to be installed in your monthly budget. This thirty-two cents per month is a very important figure.

Unless you are buying a condominium unit.

Condominium buyers and owners routinely complain about homeowners' dues, HOD, the same way professional athletes complain about the media. Both are necessary evils. HOD, in a well-run condominium, actually force you to contribute some utilities, insurance, and maintenance on a monthly basis. In many ways, if you are buying your first residence, a condo teaches you the true cost of residential home ownership. This is why you are preapproved for a lower dollar amount on a condo than on a home; the condominium homeowners' association is simply forcing you to put aside money for certain residence costs.

If you are buying a condo unit, your maintenance cost for a square footage of home ownership is probably closer to ten to fifteen cents per foot, per month, after you have paid your mortgage, taxes, and HOD.[2]

Ignoring the ongoing costs of home ownership leads to extreme, pervasive stress. If you do not have, or have not, set aside the appropriate money for these expenses, you will constantly be worried about the next inevitable home system breakdown: When there is a wind storm, you will

---

2 It is problematic and perhaps misleading to give a more precise number for condominiums.

worry about your old roof loosing shingles. When there is a snow storm, you will worry about your furnace breaking. If the weather is sunny and perfect, you might start thinking about repainting your home. If you have budgeted for these, and are prepared for them, none of them are concerns.

These two stress options, maintaining your home and not doing so, offer dichotomous outcomes for your overall quality of life and sense of contentment, especially if you have loved ones under your roof.

HOME ALONE?

So eight cents to drive a mile (in 1950!) and thirty-two cents to maintain a home. This should make you consider the size of your home.

Debating the morality of home size would yield a vast range of disparate arguments from very good people. Who is to say what the right home size is?

Certainly not me. The cost of maintaining a home, though, should make you consider your values and your allocation of resources toward supporting those values. Grandpa Herb had a home on the border of Northwestern University, in Evanston, Illinois. This is the same small city where *Home Alone* and *Uncle Buck* were filmed; there is a flat grid of tree-lined streets hosting large colonial homes. His house, including the basement, was about thirty-five hundred square feet.

Grandpa Herb had a wife and three children and a propensity to entertain. His children, including my dad, spent their entire childhoods in this home or immediately across the street at a local schoolyard. They vacationed via automobile no more than once or twice a year.

Herb got huge value from his home, as did his wife and children. He filled it with love and memories, and I think it would be hard to argue his statistically large home was immoral for its size.

His allocation of resources, though, might have been viewed differently if he lived alone, had not spent time at home, and did not dine and entertain routinely at home. As far as a primary residence goes, why would he have paid for thirty-five hundred feet he had no use for?

There's no correct answer to how large a home you should own besides your own when you are fully informed. That is your decision, and your decision alone. Hiding spare chocolate in your socks, however, is always a good idea.

13

ONE SECRET DECISION THAT DICTATES YOUR REAL-ESTATE WEALTH

There is major glaring difference between independently wealthy people and those who are not:

Nonwealthy people routinely pay independently wealthy people. That is to say, wealthy people collect money from nonwealthy people as an intelligent, strategic practice.

For example, take insurance. Any type of insurance is simply normal people paying independently wealthy people to use their money in the event of an unexpected expense. Insurance would not exist if it were a money-losing industry, or if the general public had the cash reserves to finance unexpected events. As a group of individuals, we pay more in insurance than we ever get back; otherwise, no one would offer insurance service.

When you buy a car with a loan or lease a car, someone wealthy is being paid because you did not buy the car with cash. The only reason the car is loaned to you is because a wealthy person is making money off your loan and is secured to some degree from your default.

When you rent a hotel room, you are paying a wealthy person who has the resources to own and maintain that room so that they can charge you a premium for staying in it.

What's more, in many cases, the residuals wealthy people collect off of us are passive income. That is to say that they are not putting in significant hourly work to collect the money from us.

The standard American mortgage, a thirty-year amortized loan, is a large-scale example of wealthy people collecting money from unwealthy people. By taking out a thirty-year loan, you are agreeing to a long-term rental with a wealthy person whereby you, not your landlord, maintain the home, pay taxes on it, and insure it. If you fail to pay the wealthy person for you home at any point in time, they retain the money you have paid them, and they retain your home. *(Do you think Warren Buffet uses thirty-year residential loans to finance his real estate investments?)*

What a great investment for the mortgage grantor!

If you and I had the money, we would entertain holding thirty-year mortgages as well!

I am not arguing that this practice is immoral or unintelligent, simply that the average American with a thirty-year amortization does not own their home in the pure sense of the word: you are engaged in an agreement that makes a wealthy person wealthier and gives you a slightly lower rent payment and the tasks and fees associated with home ownership. Somewhere, someone else is winning this arrangement with you, otherwise they wouldn't do it.

You don't have to let this happen. If you are competitive, this chapter is for you.

How Do I Make a Wealthy Decision?

Do you plan in staying in your current home for thirty years?

How many people do you know that plan on staying in their home for thirty years?

Most people own their homes for approximately ten years or about one-third the duration of a thirty-year mortgage.[1] The problem is that you don't make real financial gains in the first ten years of a thirty-year

---

1 The duration of home ownership varies significantly, from nine to thirteen years, depending on the source. The number ten was chosen here because home-ownership duration is decreasing, meaning future studies indicating current home-ownership duration will likely fall toward the nine-year number.

mortgage. This is the crux of this entire chapter. I suggest reading that last sentence again! Agreeing to a thirty-year mortgage is like paying for an "All You Can Eat" buffet and then eating one cup of soup:

—You will gain, approximately, 20 percent equity in your home in the first ten years of a thirty-year mortgage. This is to say, about the time most people change homes, you will still owe someone almost 80 percent of your original loan.[2]

—You will pay your lender almost twice the amount of equity you earn, $62,548 in interest, than you gain in principal payoff, in the first ten years of a thirty-year loan.[3]

—When all is said and done, the average American will have rented his or her home for $718 per month during the course of a thirty-year mortgage closed out in ten years.[4] (We will discuss true rent rates and the "rent vs. buy" question later.) To an investor, you are simply a safer renter who is guaranteeing to pay for the investor's home, or give it back. You are also paying all taxes, insurance, and maintenance on their collateral.

—Despite popular belief, the average-priced American home, using Case-Shiller statistics from the last thirty years, only increases in value 1.3 percent per year (which is better than the last ten years in which the Case-Shiller Index has shown almost no increase in real-estate values nationwide). Using this data, albeit simplified, the average American home will increase in price only $24,100 over the next ten years (The median home price according to Case-Shiller and Zillow is about $175,000).

A thirty-year mortgage, during its first ten years, is a rental with the burdens of home ownership. For lenders, it is a passive money-making venture, backed by a tangible piece of real estate they can reclaim in the event of default.

---

2 $36,890, or exactly 21.4 percent of total loan. Using Zillow median-priced American home at time of print, $178,400, purchased with an FHA 3.5 percent down-payment loan. So a loan balance of $172,135 amortized over thirty years paid back at 4 percent interest.

3 Using the same purchasing plan from footnote 2.

4 Explained in detail in "Profit of Home Ownership" chart near the end of this chapter.

HOW DO YOU ACTUALLY
OWN YOUR HOME AND LIVE FOR FREE?

Amortization is the schedule for the repayment of debt, in the case of a home mortgage, with interest. At the end of an amortization schedule, you will have paid off all of your debt, and additionally, all of the interest you agreed to pay a lender for borrowing money. Here are the amortization details for a home mortgage of $300,000 on thirty- and fifteen-year amortizations:

THIRTY-YEAR AMORTIZATION EXAMPLE:

$300,000 home loan, borrowed at 4 percent interest
$300,000 paid back to lender in thirty years
$215,609 paid to lender as interest
$515,609 in total paid for $300,000 loan
42 percent of total money paid is paid toward interest

FIFTEEN-YEAR AMORTIZATION EXAMPLE

$300,000 home loan, borrowed at 3.25 percent interest (fifteen-year amortization interest rates are generally about 0.75 percent less than thirty-year amortization interest rates)
$300,000 paid back to lender in fifteen years
$79,441 paid to lender as interest
$379,441 in total paid for $300,000 loan
21 percent of the total money paid is paid toward interest

For your mortgage, you make payments monthly to your lender, all of them the same amount over the duration of the loan. There are two portions of the payment. In the first portion, you are paying off principal of your loan, or the loan itself. In the second portion, you are paying interest on the balance you owe the lender, or profit to a lender for loaning you money.

Over the life of the loan, the amount you pay toward principal and interest changes every month. Early in the loan schedule, on a thirty-year amortization, you pay much more interest than principal:

First payment, thirty-year mortgage, on the $300,000 home:
$1,432 total payment (mortgage only, not including taxes and insurance)
$1,000 in interest paid
$432 in loan balance paid
In your first payment, 70 percent of the payment is debt service, profit, to a lender.

Last payment (at thirty years):
$5 in interest paid
$1,427 in loan balance paid

First payment, fifteen-year mortgage, on the $300,000 home above:
$2,108 total payment (mortgage only, not including taxes and insurance)
$813 in interest paid
$1,296 in loan balance paid!
In your first payment, you claim about three times the equity you would in the thirty-year amortization.

The last payment would have been made in fifteen years, not thirty.

Google "loan amortization schedule" to find an easy-to-use calculator and amortization schedule that shows you exactly how much of each payment goes in your pocket (loan balance pay down) and how much goes to a lender (interest).

As you can tell, as the thirty-year loan progresses, a higher and higher proportion of your payment is applied toward paying off your principal. But this doesn't really swing in your favor for about a decade—just about the time you will sell the home.

WHY MCDONALD'S AND TACO BELL NAPKINS MIGHT CHARACTERIZE THE MILLIONAIRE NEXT DOOR

Immediately after college, guests to my apartment in Palmdale, California, could use a nice pool, decent basketball courts, and expect to receive McDonald's napkins with meals at my house, along with McDonald's ketchup and McDonald's hot mustard. When I had my first real job, I had almost no expendable income, so I cut costs wherever I could. Real napkins and condiments in bottles were not things I afforded at that time. For most people, this is a common occurrence: your lowest income will occur in your twenties.

During this time, it is socially acceptable to live a frugal, maybe slightly uncomfortable lifestyle. Fifteen-year amortizations definitely raise your monthly payment, so this is the best time, when you buy your first home, to buy on a fifteen-year amortization and truly own your home, as opposed to signing a thirty-year rental agreement (loan).

While it costs you about $718 to rent your own home with a thirty-year amortization, you live for free, or better, with a fifteen-year amortization. Again, you are primarily paying someone else interest, paying property taxes, homeowner's insurance, and maintenance in the first ten years of a thirty-year amortization—someone is really, really, making good safe money off you. (Why do you think we get asked to refinance our homes almost daily? One main reason is for an investor to start the high interest-payment schedule over!)

> When you sell, about ten years down the road, you have created you have created $130,512 in home equity with a fifteen-year loan.

Then, in your late thirties or forties, you actually have the resources, having been stored in real estate, to make a reasonable down payment in a better neighborhood or home:

—If you bought a median-priced home, you will have over $130,000 in equity.

—If you bought a home with a mortgage value of $300,000, you will have over $227,000 in equity.

—If you bought a home with a mortgage value of $500,000, you will have over $377,602 in equity.

These simply from choosing a fifteen-year amortization.

Once out of your twenties and thirties, and beyond your first jobs, you are more likely to have a family or social life that necessitates a better neighborhood. At that age, it is less likely McDonald's napkins, and a bad neighborhood, will be palatable to you. Your first home or second home is the one you want to "rough it" in.

If you use a thirty-year mortgage for your first home, you are living in relative opulence at a time when your peers don't care, in exchange for later living at a lesser standard when your peers, and potentially children, do.

Fifteen-year amortizations, fifteen-year loans, place you immediately in the financial position of significantly paying your house down. They quickly build your cash reserves in a safe place where you won't touch it. Fifteen-year loan interest rates are generally about 25 percent less than thirty-year rates. Most importantly, they actually put you in a functional home-ownership position, as opposed to a loan amortization so long it is actually a rental.

Interest paid to investor	$62,548[5]	$40,090[6]
Closing costs to buy home	$5,164[7]	$5,164
Closing costs to sell home	$16,335[8]	$16,335

5 Median American home price at time of print, according to Zillow, is $174,800. Assuming this home is purchased with a 3.5 percent down payment FHA loan, the balance is $172,135. At 4 interest, total interest paid over ten years is $62,548.

6 Median American home price at time of print, according to Zillow, is $174,800. Assuming this home is purchased with a 3.5 percent down payment FHA loan, the balance is $172,135. At 3.25 percent interest, total interest paid over ten years is $40,090.

7 Using 3 percent closing costs generally associated with FHA loan.

8 Using closing costs in Washington State, approximately 8.25 percent, which include commissions, sales tax, title insurance, and escrow fees. Closing costs based on projected price of home in ten years, $198,900, using 1.3 percent home-price appreciation, or the average for home-price appreciation according to the Case-Schiller Index over the last thirty years.

	30-Year Mort.	15-year Mort.
Property taxes for ten years	$18,685[9]	$18,685
Homeowners insurance	$7,536[10]	$7,536
Maintenance	$28,260[11]	$28,260
Utilities	$24,492[12]	$24,492

Total costs for owning average sized American home of median value for ten years:

	30-Year Mort.	15-year Mort.
	$162,820	**$140,562**

PROFIT

	30-Year Mort.	15-Year Mort.
Equity (loan balance paid off)	**$36,890[13]**	**$106,264 (!)**
Appreciation	$24,100[14]	$24,100
Tax incentive	$15,636[15]	$10,023

TOTAL PROFIT

	30 Year	15 Year
	$76,626	$140,387 (!)

PROFIT—COST

	30-Year Mort.	15-year Mort.
	−$86,194	−$175
OR	$718 rent per month	$1.46 rent per month

9 One percent property tax rate.

10 Using 1,570-square-foot home. Insurance cost of four cents per square foot per month taken from the 2015 Consumer Expenditures Survey (CE) published by the Bureau of Labor Statistics.

11 Using 1,570-square-foot home. Maintenance cost of fifteen cents per square foot per month taken from the 2015 Consumer Expenditures Survey (CE) published by the Bureau of Labor Statistics.

12 Using 1,570-square-foot home. Utilities cost of thirteen cents per square foot per month for gas, electricity, water, and trash taken from the 2015 Consumer Expenditures Survey (CE) published by the Bureau of Labor Statistics.

13 Equity gained off home mortgage amount $172,135 after ten years, 4 percent interest.

14 1.3 percent appreciation, or average yearly appreciation using Case-Shiller Index over last thirty years.

15 Tax write-off in 25 percent tax bracket on total of $62,548 mortgage interest paid

Buy Versus Rent?

The average US rent is $962.

In this example, at approximately five years, an average rental home, and a home bought on a thirty-year amortization would have cost about the same amount of money. Said again, using this example, if you lived somewhere less than five years a rental and home ownership with a thirty-year amortization would have been the same, financially speaking.

This is to say nothing of time—the only truly priceless resource you actually own.

If you have owned a home, you know the sense of security if offers, particularly, as your domestic unit grows in size. You also know how much time and stress goes into owning a home. While economists can and do measure and quantify the value of time and stress, only one measurement matters: yours.

Here are the true rules of owning versus renting:

—The best answer is yours, and yours alone. It is subjective to your needs, preferences, and desires only. There is no shame in buying versus renting, indeed many renters are smarter than owners. Buying can create wealth, but doesn't necessarily.

—Your considerations should include financial, but also—and equally important—time, freedom, and general well-being as measured in stress. If you have children, do you want them to feel grounded (owning)? If you have no children, how important is it to be able to turn the lights off and leave at any time, not worrying about maintenance (renting)?

—It makes more sense to buy the longer you plan on living somewhere, particularly over five years. But this is tricky, because at the end of the day, we have little control over our jobs, our relationships, and the health of our family.

—Thirty-year amortizations are far less preferable to fifteen-year amortizations. Far less. Fifteen-year amortizations are much more likely to create wealth and allow for freedom of lifestyle. This decision is one of the most, if not the most, important primary-residence real-estate decisions you will ever make in your first or second home. You will hear many say, when choosing a thirty-year amortization, "I like to keep my cash in hand." What this really means is they don't have any cash, or they leverage most of it. Fifteen-year amortizations force you to save, thirty-year amortizations leave cash in your hands to spend, usually on noninterest bearing consumer items.

—If you buy, use a conventional loan and put 20 percent down. You will avoid mortgage insurance and allow yourself the freedom to reanalyze your home, location, and happiness at any day during your home ownership. This is not true if you, for example, use an FHA loan and put 3.5 percent down: on day 1, considering closing costs, you already have negative equity in your own home.

It would be very, very difficult to "lose" on real estate if you put 20 percent down and used a fifteen-year amortization: you receive the lowest interest rate, avoid mortgage insurance, pay your home off quickly, and have equity sufficient to move under any circumstances. Saving 20 percent, too, teaches you to budget before making the biggest purchase of your life. Many people say "keep your cash in hand," with regard to using low down payment, thirty-year amortizations. Ask those same people if they could move tomorrow, if they wanted to, after investing in and working on the largest financial commitment of their life.

14

WHY YOU SHOULD ABANDON A HOUSING BUDGET AND ADOPT A LIFESTYLE BUDGET

I loathe gardening, but I love gardens, and I have two beautiful gardens. I cannot bear gardening, but I love gardens.

—SIR ELTON JOHN

You have a limited amount of monthly income—not wealth, not "net worth," but income. Just consider your monthly income—the resources you use to live off of every month. Imagine this income in a watering can. Imagine, also, you have a landscape, a garden, to cultivate with this one watering can every month. The garden is all the things you could devote resources to in your life.

There is only so much water in this can to pour out. You can distribute the water however you want every month, but there is only so much of it, and your garden relies on this amount of water to live.

Americans who own homes pour about one-third of their water every month on "housing."[1]

Americans spend about one-third of

their income (gross income) on housing, not including home maintenance or furnishings. As an example, an American who makes $6,000 a month, $72,000 per year, spends approximately $2,000 a month in mortgage or rent.[2] This portion of their income keeps a roof over their heads. It doesn't keep them warm or fed, but it keeps a structure protecting them.

Up to one-third of this $6,000 monthly income, or approximately another $2,000 a month, goes toward income taxes and basic housing maintenance, furnishings, and utilities.

So at the end of the month, the individual in this example has fixed costs for the month, costs they cannot change, of about two-thirds their income, or about $4,000. On the first day of every month, many Americans pour two-thirds of their water supply out immediately on their home, and to the IRS. For a roof over your head, a warm home, and basic tax liability, most people are spending about two-thirds of their income, emptying about two-thirds of their watering can.

This leaves one-third a can for every other pursuit that month.

The water that is left over, the final one-third, has to propagate:

—Food
—Education
—Health care
—Travel
—Entertainment
—Debt service
—Investments
—Gifts
—Fitness
—Other

The problem with the water used for the first two-thirds of your budget, is that it "waters" things that don't necessarily make you happy. The first two-thirds of the watering can sustain your lawn. They don't grow strawberries, dahlias, or apple trees. You can easily pour out $4,000 a month keeping your mortgage holder and the IRS happy, but still be house poor. Your lender and the government are satisfied, but the rest of

2 This figure is a sound estimation but is only an estimation. Allotment of monthly income for various budgetary needs varies widely across income and demographic characteristics.

your garden may be drying up; savings, investments, fitness, education, and travel.

It's very possible to work forty to sixty hours per week, pay for housing, pay your taxes, and be generally unhealthy and dissatisfied with your life. You could even live in a wonderful home, nicer than one you had ever imagined living in, and be generally depressed, stressed, and overwhelmed.

It is highly unlikely you will be dissatisfied with your life if the nonfixed portion of your budget is poured on healthy food, meaningful education, good preventative health care, regular travel, and stimulating entertainment. These things would all be symptoms of a vibrant dynamic life. Additionally, if good money from this one-third of the nonfixed portion of your budget goes toward simple, sound, and satisfying financial investments, your confidence in your current lifestyle, and future one, will be high and subsequently chronic stress level low.

The problem with the fixed allocations of your budget, housing and taxes, are that they are fixed! You really don't have a choice about where to pour this portion of your budget once you decide on your home. Under normal circumstances (2008 and 2009 were not normal!), these expenditures are fixed in stone; you have to make these payments every month.

The nonfixed portion of your budget can be distributed as you please, watered where you desire. Inevitably, though, there are portions of your garden, parched, that scream out for immediate water from this discretionary one-third:

—Health emergencies
—House emergencies
—Car trouble
—Family members in need
—Unexpected expenditures

If your refrigerator breaks, do you use your remaining water to replace it or pay for a health club, nourishing food, and a vacation?

Everyone buys the refrigerator in this case. Buying a refrigerator, though, has little or no positive impact on your life's trajectory.

We all need to pour some water on the parts of our gardens that make us happy. This allocation of resources is a lifestyle budget: it's the fruit of your labors. This lifestyle budget should be made nonnegotiable, like your mortgage or rent, to maximize your life.

GROWING A VACATION

Vacation, travel, is part of your garden that you can ignore, but shouldn't. It's every bit as vital to your health as diet and fitness. Vacation makes you healthy. In many ways, the benefits of vacation are more imminently and obviously rewarding than anything you could eat or any workout you could do.

How do you feel when you get home from a ten-day vacation without your phone?

We are far better at marketing vacations than actually taking them. Modern Americans take less vacation time than any group of our predecessors. The amount of vacation time used by Americans is almost a full week less than the amount of paid vacation time available. We work almost fifty weeks and then forego a week off? This is preposterous! Over 85 percent of Americans will not take a trip of greater than two weeks this year, and trips this long are exactly what we need.

Can you remember what you were doing at this time last week? Yesterday? Can you name an important life event that occurred to you last month at work? It's hard to do! The sad truth is that most of our year is highly forgettable. Recently, we made a list of our five favorite memories from 2014. All five of them were when on vacation.

We Americans get conditioned in our daily work paths, like ants in an ant farm, and then carry the same little white rocks to the same places day after day. This is something nonhuman that animals do well. It is not something that makes humans happy, even though we can easily revert to this animal state.

What separates us from animals, our consciousness, is maximized by stimulation and variation. Travel and vacation instill these feelings and subsequently maximize our lives and consciousness. Many individuals report life-changing events and epiphanies on vacations.

Without dynamic changing circumstance in our lives, we are really just grooving tracks in an ant farm, not many days distinguishable from the others. Ironically though, our work lives and our personal lives improve with regular vacation away from them: taking time off work makes you a better worker.

Travel is proven to be every bit as beneficial as fitness and diet to your overall health. Chronic and acute illness, stress and depression are all scientifically proven to occur less, or to a lesser degree, to people who routinely vacation.

As people, why are we giving our employers free work days and running our physical and emotional selves into the ground? Where is the pot of gold at the end of this rainbow? If you are proactive about having a meaningful life, you will vacation regularly and vigorously. What can you do to make sure your housing choice doesn't put you in a small plastic ant farm?

Abandon your housing budget and adopt a lifestyle budget.

What is a lifestyle budget?

It could be explained in two parts:

1. It is pouring the first portion of your monthly water on the parts of the garden that create a meaningful life for you and your loved ones.
2. It is decreasing the amount of water you have to pour on fixed expenditures every month.

A lifestyle budget grows your own happy garden.

If you make only housing and taxes a priority, at the end of the year, you will have a roof over your head and a general propensity to daydream about harming members of the IRS. Hopefully, you want more than this!

I recently helped a school teacher implement a lifestyle budget. After eight months, she had allocated $10,000 cash for a house down payment, vacations, gifts, her future wedding, and an extended adventure in California. Additionally, she maxed out her IRA contributions for this time period. This is a teacher who designed a lifestyle budge on a spreadsheet. Every time she made money, down to the dollar, she allocated it in distinct percentage allotments.

If she made one hundred dollars, it was predetermined where the money would go, down to the dollar. All of the money went to one bank account, but she kept a spreadsheet on Google Drive that she could access daily and update.

Most importantly, she reported to me, almost weekly, with a glowing smile her totals for each category. Now, eighteen months later, she is a teacher who can grow more than she ever thought possible in her own garden (prior to the eighteen months, she used a similar process to pay off six years of college, including a master's degree, and credit-card debt).

Your monthly allocation for fixed housing expenses should become a monthly investment in housing, savings, investment, and health. If you can guarantee your rent will be paid, you can also guarantee the controllable portions of your future that dictate your day-to-day happiness. Your lifestyle budget does not need to be the same as your housing budget was; the important thing is to allocate your monthly income to nonnegotiable categories.

Here is an example:

Housing budget of $2,000:
Mortgage—$2,000

Lifestyle budget of $2,500:
Housing—$1,750
Extra investment—$150
Two gym memberships—$100
Healthy food premium (no more McDonald's once/week, instead, Whole Foods salad bar)—$25
Travel—$300
Weekly massage for back pain—$175

This can be set up easily by creating a spreadsheet on Google Drive.

When you get paid, simply allocate money in your predetermined amounts to each category. Again, these are categories that you have determined to be vital to your fullest life. They are a personal conviction that you will take the simple steps necessary to make sure your vacations, and emergency appliance replacements, occur. Without a lifestyle budget, you will constantly react to inevitable financial demands of living and working and simply forego your important categories.

This practice has the unintended effect of also building small budgetary accounts of extra money; if you get to the end of a year, you would find you probably have extra money in some of these accounts. At that point, you can redistribute your own wealth, splurge, or invest the money. Without having made a lifestyle budget, it is more likely you will end up looking for more money for the latest "emergency" in December, and putting everyone's Christmas gift on your credit card.

For most people, housing costs are at least twice as much as any other category of spending in the domestic unit. Sadly, when we take on bigger house payments, though, we cut important pieces of our budget out. First among these are gym memberships. Gym memberships get cut because they are easily recognizable as money saving cost cuts.

Cell phone bills aren't considered the same way; we can't just discontinue cell service. Cable bills are seemingly small, and cable TV seemingly necessary. Saving money on utilities is challenging to plan and execute.

So, what goes? Gym memberships. Cut. They are like an aging all-star at the end of an NBA contract—an easy way to shave some cap room.

This could all be saved by having a lifestyle budget before you engage in your next housing choice. You can afford the gym, probably easily, but you need to be prepared with a plan for how you are going to afford it. Without this, it's simply too easy to cut!

Most of our parents, and grandparents, and great grandparents advised us to invest in real estate. They were right and we should. What they meant, though, was to invest in real estate as part of a larger portfolio of wealth. If you are seeing your home as a sole savings and investment plan, you are fooling yourself as to the legitimacy of your future wealth for several reasons:

First, the market has shown us over time, particularly over periods of less than five years that real-estate prices fluctuate drastically. What if you have to sell, for a job relocation, to have access to a hospital, or to get closer to a dying loved one? What if the market is down when you have to move? You just spent your savings plan.

Second, when people do realize wealth as a result of selling real estate, they may not have the discipline to reallocate this money to other solid investments. It feels like a windfall, which could easily go toward a car and another home, and then be gone. This windfall can be easily spent and then leveraged onto more debt.

Finally, it exposes you to the risk of a financial portfolio legitimized by only one category. People think they will "hit it big" in real estate, buying to their max. The amount of money devoted to the mortgage, taxes, insurance, and maintenance is maxed out. What happens if the real-estate market dictates this investment "down" when you try to sell?

How hard would it be to make your housing payments if the primary income earner in your domestic unit lost his or her job? What if both income earners lost their jobs?

The reality of any economy is dynamic behavior, changing behavior, which is always in flux. When things start to get "bad," they tend to move in a "bad" direction; the possibility that one or more income earners could lose their job, and take a long time to get another job, increases as the events occur. When economies trend downward, most market segments are adversely affected, threatening many people's jobs or pay scale.

How long could you make your payments if you had no income? Would it force you to go to your parents?

The perceived safety net that parental lending and giving offers is an emotionally and functionally damaging occurrence. For starters, it draws on your confidence to beg your parents for money. Worse, how do the other siblings in your family feel about you taking preferential payments from your parents? Inevitably, it causes sad and damaging family rifts.

"But I never thought it would get to this, it was an honest mistake."

No, it wasn't. The economy will change, your job status and pay will change, your health status will change. These are the simple honest truths about adult life. When these changes occur, are you left kneeling at your parents' doorstep for bread? Are you forced into negotiating debt forgiveness with banks, the IRS, or private parties?

Ultimately, if you cannot be responsible for yourself, you cannot create and enjoy the possibilities of a fulfilled life; key among this equation is challenge and honesty, and these are things you can control before buying a home that would make you a beggar when the economy inevitably changes.

15

CHILD LABOR

E ver wonder where Michael Jordan developed the habit of sticking out his tongue while he made aggressive plays in the NBA? Jordan says it came from his dad, who stuck his tongue out when he worked.

Where did Jordan's dad get it? From watching his dad work.

Teaching your children how to work is a lesson that will benefit them throughout their lives. Having a good work ethic enables children to study and achieve in school and to feel competent and self-sufficient. A strong work ethic also is key to their future success in the workplace.

—RICHARD BROMFIELD, PHD [1]

We'd all love to pass on Hall of Fame basketball pedigree to our sons. Easier though, and more important, is a work ethic.

We don't see our dad or mom work anymore. In most cases, they leave in the morning, come home at night, hopefully eat dinner with us, and

1 Richard Bromfield, "Family," Parade Magazine, July 26, 1990.

then put us to bed. Many parents lead a white-collar work life that offers no tangible trail of work for their children to see. Additionally, perhaps more importantly, domestic units have smaller yards and spend less time tending their yards themselves. And by enlarge, the American middle class has become a service hiring economic phenomena; we hire out everything, from our furnace maintenance to our manicures. This was not true even thirty years ago.

It's possible that the majority of forthcoming generations will not actually see either of their parents ever complete physical "work."

They may see them leave and come home but not actually put a shovel in soil or apply paint to a building.

A good work attitude develops from years of age-appropriate opportunity and responsibility that begins at home. Here are some ways for parents to instill a healthy work ethic in their children:

Start early. Young children love to help their parents. Encourage them to do so. Let their little hands share the dust mop handle or the hammer.

Teach. Find ways that your children can assist in housework or a do-it-yourself project. Remember, the goal isn't to get a good day's labor out of them, but to nurture their work attitudes and make them feel able, to grow their confidence.

Have expectations. Even very young children can contribute to a household. Whatever their age, expect every child to play a role. Putting away toys, setting the table or raking leaves are examples of tasks that children can do.

—BROMFIELD

The single most common personality trait of highly successful people, according to Napoleon Hill, author of Think and Grow Rich, is persistence. The sheer capacity to keep going, in spite of setbacks, pain, embarrassment, physical duress, and disillusionment. Persistence.

Persistence isn't something children can read about in a book or be taught by a teacher. It is formed of drive and example, the example of people children look up to around them. Physical labor is the most basic, primal teacher of persistence.

Modern families tend to ascribe to one of three trends with regard to yard work nowadays:

Buy a home without a yard.

Buy a home with a yard but defer maintenance.

Buy a home with a yard and hire the work out.

What does a child turn into who has never significantly completed a manual labor task, much less a full day of physical manual labor?

First, they are far more likely to be unfit, overweight, or inactive.

Second, they have missed the formative universal experience of work: to identify a job and complete it.

Third, they have no recollection or concept of manual labor so they will have a difficult time relating to people whom they are asking to accomplish feats later.

The answer, the solution, to teaching persistence through work is not illegally mandating full workdays of child labor. You can, though, make work and persistence a habit with simple household chores, and through shared labor. It is very important that your children see you working.

ONE SEAMLESS WAY TO WORK IS TO GARDEN.

The benefits of tangible outdoor gardens, not necessarily on your property, are proven and documented, applicable at all income levels and to all demographics.

Neighborhood gardens with active participation drastically increase the aesthetic of a community, including the condition of homes. Neighborhoods are safer, houses nicer, with neighborhood gardens.

A working garden at your own home increases your fitness, can positively impact your diet, and has quantifiable stress reducing qualities for the people who work in it. Some studies show that yard work qualifies as moderate to heavy physical labor that counts toward your daily fitness and activity goals.

Gardens don't have to be large, fancy, or even highly productive to pass on these benefits, but you do have to be working them actively. Gardens also provide hands on education for your children, with first hand experiential knowledge about biology, weather, energy, and even math.

Even if you have waning interest in gardening activities, all you would have to do to sustain your interest in a garden is take your child to it daily to witness the growing power of nature. Witnessed daily, an active garden is every bit as entertaining, and more physically active, than television.

16

HOW MUCH TIME DOES YOUR REAL ESTATE COST?

The single thing you will notice most about your home is the amount of time you put into it.

The average person spends about one-third of their income on their mortgage,[1] but no one sits at work and thinks, "Goodness, I wish I didn't have to work the first three hours of the day to put a roof over my head."

Once you have made your mortgage payment, it is gone and forgotten. Your roof, your lawn, your carpets, and your bathrooms are not—almost everyone who owns a home, even those who hire the maintenance out for their home, think about the maintenance of their home weekly, if not daily.

Men spend about an hour a day tending to their homes, and women spend two hours—per day, not per week.[2] This means an average couple is spending fifteen to twenty hours per week on their home: housework, landscaping, and household management. This does not include food preparation or cleanup. An average couple will spend another one and

---

1 US Bureau of Labor Statistics, 2015.

2 Ibid.

one-half hours or so shopping for goods and services per day, many of these residing in, or relating to, the home. This is over ten hours per week shopping.

In fact buying a home, particularly with a mortgage, is as much a "time" agreement as it is a "financial one":

> —*Many consider real-estate transactions in the top three of stressors—death, divorce, and real estate.* Shopping for a home, going through the escrow process on a home, and then closing on a home are time consuming. Once you have gone through this three to twelve month process, you are unlikely to engage in it again soon.
>
> —*Almost no one truly likes moving, and most people hate it.* Moving into a home, with all of your belongings, is a time-consuming and potentially physically demanding task. Generally speaking, we try to minimize our "moves."
>
> —*Once you and your loved ones move into a home, you develop a real emotional relationship with the place and the home itself.* This is a measurable emotional bond that you don't want to break if you don't have a strong motivator to do so. As a result, it is emotionally hard to move, or to tell your loved ones they need to pack up and move with you. These emotions extend to neighbors or neighborhood animals you and your loved ones may become fond of.
>
> —*If you buy with a low down payment (3.5 percent), you won't have enough profit to move for three to five years (closing costs to move are about 8.25 percent).* The profits realized on your primary-residence real estate take years to accumulate.
>
> —Affording the "hiring" of home maintenance is not as easy as it might seem. *Inevitably, some of the workers or jobs are substandard at best and criminal at worst.* Hiring home service, as opposed to doing it yourself, is potentially as time consuming. Finding workers, booking workers, and meeting workers for your home projects is a bona fide managerial task. Once subcontractors start working on your home, you must negotiate and enforce contracts, manage the quality of the work, and supervise the completion of the work.

So when you sign closing paperwork on a home, you are obviously signing a financial agreement, but what's more important and noticeable in your day-to-day life is that you are signing a "time" agreement. Function-ally, you are agreeing to years of financial responsibility, residence, maintenance, and emotional concern for your home.

There is endless money in the world, but you have limited time, the amount of which is unknown. Our government proves this when they print more money. By definition, your time is priceless! This doesn't occur to most of us until the middle one-third of our lives, but when it does, it smacks us across the face, jolting us awake. If people enjoyed devoting hours a day to their homes, they would never downsize. But, as people, we do downsize; once you have owned a large home, you are very likely to buy a smaller one, on a more manageable lot in the future. Not many of our parents say, "I wish I had a much bigger home and bigger yard to maintain."

HOBBITON, SHIRE, NEW ZEALAND
The Hobbit House: an extreme case of downsizing!

How do I make a good time decision?

If you are about to sign up for a time agreement, a mortgage, congratulations! Your home will set the backdrop for years of joyful living, and here are several major factors that guarantee these years stay joyful. They are followed by scores 1, 2, and 3, so you can mark whether each item will have a low, moderate, or high time burden in your life. At the end of the section, you can add and analyze your score.

1. Commute: The average one-way commute is twenty-five minutes.[3] Commuting has legitimate detrimental physiological impacts on women, much more so than men.[4] What is your commute?

    1. 0–20 minutes
    2. 20–30 minutes
    3. 30+ minutes

2. Home Size: One square foot of average American housing costs thirty-two cents per square foot per month to own and maintain.[5] Do you have the right amount of space for the people in your home such that you are not devoting undue time to household tasks and management?

    1. 0–500 sq. ft./person
    2. 500–800 sq. ft./person
    3. 800 + sq. ft./person

3. Construction Age: Here is your argument to buy a new home! Newer construction is far easier and less costly to maintain. Particularly, homes built in the last ten years with cement board siding, vinyl windows, and gabled roofs with composite shingles.

    1. 0–10-year-old construction
    2. 10–30-year-old construction
    3. 30+ year-old construction

4. Proximity to Primary Leisure Activities (Fitness): When you place your home in a Google map, how many leisure/fitness opportunities exist within a given radius of your home? If your favorite activities are at the boundary line of how far you will drive to do them, it's taking you significant time simply to get to the location of the activity. A good example would be a tennis club or driving range if you are a tennis or golf athlete.

    1. 0–10 minutes' drive
    2. 10–20 minutes' drive

3 U.S. Census Bureau, 2009-2013 5-Year American Community Survey, Economic Characteristics p.137.

4 Jennifer Robertsa, Robert Hodgsona, and Paul Dolanb, "'It's Driving Her Mad': Gender Differences in the Effects of Commuting on Psychological Health," Journal of Health Economics 30, no. 5 (September 2011): 1064–76.

5 Median home size, 1,570 square feet. Median home price, $174,800 (Zillow). Thirty-year amortized FHA loan at 4 percent interest with mortgage balance of $172,135. Mortgage + property taxes + homeowners insurance + gas heat + electricity + trash + water + maintenance (Bureau of Labor Statistics).

3. 20+ minutes' drive

5. Proximity to Preferred Grocery Shopping: Can you pick up food easily on the way home from work? From your workout? If you need several distinct grocery items, how far do you have to go?

1. 0–5 minutes' drive
2. 5–15 minutes' drive
3. 15+ minutes' drive

6. Landscaping: Whether you do this yourself, or hire it out, mowing your lawn is something that's only fun so many times. Landscaping, to include sweeping, raking, driveway maintenance, sport court maintenance, and any natural or artificial feature outside of your home requires time. Landscaping is directly proportional to lot size. What is your lot size?

1. 0–5,000 sq. ft.
2. 5,000–10,000 sq. ft.
3. 10,000 + sq. ft.

7. Social Connectivity: If you live in a condo, you have to spend a little time every day chatting, greeting, and glad handing some of your neighbors every day. Inevitably, you get asked to participate in community matters. On the other hand, if you live in a cul-de-sac on the edge of a ravine or greenbelt, you may seldom deal with neighbors. How often do you engage in conversation with your neighbors?

1. Daily
2. Weekly
3. Monthly or less

Total Score: (add all seven numbers together) _____
Less than 10—You have a lot of free time to do with what you please.
11–14—You have about the same amount of time as your neighbors, but you definitely feel like you spend good time on home related activities.
15+—You are swamped and really excited to get a simpler living situation at some point!

A large portion of your time gets poured into your family and vocations, health, and to some extent friends and hobbies. All of these involve creative, dynamic, and largely interpersonal pursuits. They are directly relatable to our degree of satisfaction with a life well lived and worthy of memory.

But how much of your time are you devoting to inanimate, fabricated consumable goods? What is the right amount of time in your life that should be devoted to waxing your car, maintaining your hardwood floors, or polishing your statues?

How big of a home do you have time for? How nice of a home? How much time do you want to spend maintaining, or managing the maintenance of, real estate? Are you devoting your life to the service of your loved ones, or your material possessions?

There are no right answers to these questions; the answers are truly yours to give. The answers, though, may be some of the most important you give with respect to how much time you have for the vital parts of life. What you call the vital parts of life will dictate your reflective satisfaction of your life's adventure.

The average American commute is twenty-three minutes. Women suffer the effects of commuting worse than men, particularly the stress component. In fact, among common activities, commuting is women's least favorite activity (sex is their favorite).[6] This is thought to stem from their more active duties as domestic caretakers than men.[7]

Both sexes, though, experience higher cholesterol, more chronic pain, and increased obesity with increased commuting times by nonactive forms of commuting.[8] About one-third of commuters with a daily commute of at least ninety minutes experience chronic neck and back problems.[9] The number of miles you drive may be

---

6 "Developments in the Measurement of Subjective Well-Being," Journal of Economic Per-spectives 20, no. 1 (Winter 2006): 3–24.

7 Jennifer Roberts*, Robert Hodgson, and Paul Dolan, "It's Driving Her Mad: Gender Differences in the Effects of Commuting on Psychological Well-being," Sheffield Economic Research Paper Series, SERP Number: 2009009, *Department of Economics University of Sheffield (May 2009).

8 Gallup Well-Being, "Wellbeing Lower Among Workers With Long Commutes," August 13, 2010. http://www.gallup.com/poll/142142/wellbeing-lower-among-workers-long-commutes.aspx.

9 Ibid.

the single biggest factor related to obesity.[10]

Here's a fun link to commute times in your locale:

http://project.wnyc.org/commute-times-us/embed.
html#4.00/39.06/-100.40

The type of traffic you experience during your commute is important too. If you experience light, moving, and predictable traffic, the commute is more enjoyable and bearable than unpredictable, car-clogged commutes.

Vehicle traffic times, given current technology, are unlikely to decrease in the foreseeable future, so it's worth considering your commute and who in your family has to make it.

Sorry, guys; you may have to do the driving.

10 "The Link Between Obesity and the Built Environment. Evidence from an Ecological Analysis of Obesity and Vehicle Miles of Travel in California," Health & Place 12, no. 4 (December 2006): 656–64.

17

WHAT IS THE MOST VALUABLE MATERIAL POSSESSION YOU WILL EVER OWN?

Would you rather have a one-hundred-square-foot office (10' × 10') or a ninety-square-foot office (10' × 9') and ten fine steak dinners a month? One square foot (1) in the office of your home, per month, costs roughly the equivalent of a full filet-mignon dinner, with sides, at the finest steakhouse in your city.

Research indicates that an average American may get up to (approximately) eight times more value out of the square footage in their kitchen than the square footage in any other room of their house.[1]

—We pay about $6.73 for a day of kitchen space use (waking hours only). This is an estimated cost for kitchen square footage use—the kitchen room itself—based on the total price of your home.
—For other space, including the office, we pay up to $51.06 for a day's use. One square foot in your master suite, your office, or a dining room costs you over fifty dollars per day use, per month.

---

1 Based on Time Use Survey iby Jeanne E. Arnold et al. in, Life at Home in the Twenty-First Century: 32 Families Open Their Doors (Los Angeles, CA: The Cotsen Institute of Archaeology Press, July 12, 2012).

Men wear their underwear until it absolutely disintegrates.

—JERRY SEINFELD, ON *SEINFELD*

You could be like a lot of people, having a hooded sweatshirt worn so thin your friends can see through it. Veritable, indispensable, almost a living relic of your college days—a sweatshirt so soft there's no way a manufacturer could replicate it.

Maybe it's not a sweatshirt; maybe it's a pair of jeans. Maybe it's a pair of board shorts or even a favorite old cotton T-shirt. It could be a piece of clothing that comes to mind as your favorite, one that you almost consider a family member.

Additionally, you probably have twenty-five to one hundred articles of clothing, or more, that you never wear, and you never will. These sit in your closet, or in boxes, or even at your parents' house; still, you cannot bring yourself to give these articles away, sell them, or even simply throw them out.

The threadbare sweatshirt, seemingly made more of memories than cotton, cost you a negligible amount of money per use. If you paid fifty dollars for the sweatshirt and have worn it five hundred times, the cost per use is next to nothing. This was a "good buy":

$50 purchase of favorite sweatshirt
500 uses =
10 cents per use

With regard to this sweatshirt or your favorite article of clothing, the cost per use is negligible.

Conversely, the clothing you have seldom worn and never will was a waste of money. No matter what you paid for it, the cost to you is very, very high. An uncomfortable sweatshirt bought for the same price, fifty dollars, and worn ten times costs five dollars per use:

$50 purchase of seldom used clothing
10 uses =
$5 per use

In this example, you receive fifty times more value out of your favorite sweatshirt than you do out of the clothing you really don't like:

In a perfect financial world, you wouldn't buy clothing that was fifty times less valuable than clothing you would actually wear. The purchase of the clothes you don't use and do not receive high value out of is, rationally speaking, pointless. To a large degree, though, this is hard to avoid with clothing: you don't really know, until you start wearing your clothes, which were tailored to your body and lifestyle and which don't look or feel great.

It's not hard to predict how you will use your housing, though. Good research indicates which rooms are valuable and which ones are wasted. Your home is a sweatshirt you want to fit, because it costs about fifty thousand times more.

Median home size—1,550 sq. ft.[2]
Median home value—$178,400[3]
Kitchen size, percentage of home, new construction—11.6 percent[4]
Approximate kitchen size of median home—180 sq. ft.[5] (or twelve by eighteen feet)

Example Mortgage for Median Home
Thirty-year mortgage, 4 percent interest rate
20 percent down—$35,680
Mortgage amount—$142,720
Monthly mortgage payment, with taxes, and insurance—$867 per month

Kitchen cost per month, mortgage payment—$101[6]

Other space, cost per month, mortgage payment—$766[7]

50 percent Kitchen Use Example, using thirty days per month
Monthly mortgage paid for kitchen/days per month in kitchen = $101/15 = $6.73 for a day's use of your kitchen
Monthly mortgage paid for other space/days per month in other space = $766/15 = $51.06 for a day's use of other space in your home

$51.06/$6.73 = eight times (7.587 times) the value of other rooms in the home.

Even if you use your kitchen less than average people, you would still

2 Zillow, March 2015.

3 Zillow Home Value Index, March 2015.

4 National Association of House Builders (NAHB)/Wells Fargo Housing Market Index, June 2013.

5 Zillow median home size, March 2015 × 11.6%. Kitchen size from NAHB/Wells Fargo Housing Market Index, June 2013. Author's note—Kitchen size should be considered an approximation of median kitchen size. Generally, kitchen sizes in and of themselves are not accurately, widely, and repeatedly recorded and reported. This specific figure used for illustrative purposes only.

6 Example monthly mortgage payment × 11.6 percent.

7 Example monthly mortgage payment × 88.4 percent (approximate size of the rest of the home, not including the kitchen).

get a much, much greater value out of it than the other rooms of your home. Your kitchen is the single most valuable space you will own in what is likely the biggest investment of money and time you will make in your life. Your kitchen may likely be the most valuable material possession you ever buy. It is highly unlikely you will regret choosing real estate with a kitchen that will enhance your lifestyle.

That is the paragraph you want to show your significant other when you are fighting about what to spend on a kitchen remodel, or how to buy a nice kitchen.

THE JONESES ONLY GO IN YOUR KITCHEN— SO HAVE A NICE ONE!

If you are trying to keep up with the Joneses, pay attention to which rooms in your home they actually go in! For most Americans, there is a strong subconscious (direct) association with their home size and their worth—not their financial worth, but their actual worth as a human being, as if this is measured by some government agency somewhere:

Bigger, better home = more important person.

Bigger, better home = more successful person.

Bigger, better home = smarter, better-looking person.

Our most basic human emotional need, to be recognized, can temporarily be satisfied by nicer homes and nicer material things. To some degree, everyone feels this. It is a valid human emotion that's important to heed to at some level.

If you move into an upper middle-class neighborhood, with its curving streets brimming with daisies and women running in Lululemon pants, you can't just buy a piece of land and put a mobile home on it. This would be socially unacceptable to an uncomfortable degree.

Doing this might save you money, but it would make you feel unwelcome in your own home. Your spouse, family members, and even pets would simply suffer too many unnecessary social obstacles. It wouldn't be worth proving the point of simplicity; your spouse would constantly face awkward questions in the school pickup line.

If you are going to socially stratify yourself with your real estate, and we all feel obligated to, do so in the kitchen. This is the room you will enjoy, your friends will actually see, and where most of your interpersonal memories will occur. Compete in the kitchen, because it's more effective, less costly, and more enjoyable than owning too much square footage that you won't use.

Generally, smaller dwellings with large, open kitchens make people happier in their homes. Just ask any high net-worth individual between the ages of forty and sixty who is retiring and looking for a new home. That person will not usually tell you he or she is looking for more square footage but for better square footage—square footage to use with little maintenance, and use happily.

"Downsizing" is often spoken of with a noticeable twinge of guilt; people seem reluctant, sad, or scared to "downsize" or admit that they are doing it:

"Yes, it's time for us to downsize."

The reality is different—most people are happy in smaller homes, on smaller lots, with less to worry about.

The true hurdle is social: "If I live in a smaller home, people will think less of me."

This hurdle is more easily cleared as people age, mature, and feel more comfortable and confident. Younger people, naturally, are trying to prove themselves; a big, nice house is one perceived way to do this.

Why do we finance and commit time to square footage our important friends and peers will not see? It's one thing to buy a sweatshirt that rubs the back of your neck the wrong way. With regards to a home, the purchase has much larger implications: we are talking about inventorying hundreds or thousands of square feet of physical structure that require vigilant and ongoing maintenance.

Americans may spend about one-half of their waking time in their home in the kitchen, or in the room immediately adjoining the kitchen. This is not an argument to ask your spouse to sleep on the kitchen floor. This is a finding, however, that should cause you to consider both the importance of your kitchen and the overall size of your optimal home. Most people would love to have a gourmet kitchen with vaulted ceilings in an open floor plan. Most people should, if given the chance, take this over a bonus room, huge master suite, and especially an extra bedroom.

Consider the following when looking for a new home or when looking into changing your kitchen:

— **What might you be trading for a better kitchen?** Are you trading a large home for one with a nicer kitchen? Are you trading for more rooms, as opposed to ones you will use? Is the finish level of the unused rooms in your home too high for their actual use?

— **Is the kitchen acceptable as it is?** If not, can it be easily improved? Kitchen remodels can cost from $20,000 to $300,000. Will you have to move walls, pour new foundation, and elevate ceiling height (all relatively expensive) to make your kitchen acceptable to you and to your peers?

— **How big is the kitchen, or how potentially big can the kitchen be?** If the median kitchen size is about twelve by eighteen feet, or two hundred square feet, is the kitchen you are considering comparable to this, smaller, or larger?

— **What year construction is your home?**
  • Year 2015 new construction tends to have large kitchens.
  • Midcentury homes, homes built in or near the 1950s, can have good-sized kitchens or large kitchen capacity.
  • Homes built before 1950 tend to have smaller kitchens.
  • Homes built in the 1970s and 1980s tend to have kitchens that are difficult to expand due to the location of load-bearing walls and ceiling height.

— **What is the exposure from the kitchen?** In the room you will spend the largest percentage of your waking hours at home, where do the windows look? As you learned in a preceding chapter, what you see through your kitchen windows and what color that view is can have profound, meaningful effects on your health.

—From where is the kitchen entered with regard to access by whoever carries groceries? Is the kitchen on the main level or upstairs? Is there a natural path to the refrigerator from the car, or one that makes grocery handling a hassle?

The kitchen, for the vast majority of us, is the common high-traffic intersection of our domestic lives. It doesn't seem to matter if your family prepares meals from scratch or not; most families do large amounts of planning, chatting, and studying in the kitchen. The kitchen bar has become the virtual campfire of our domestic units.

Cave paintings of our ancestors show humans around campfires.

The cave paintings drawn of our culture in the future will show us around homework projects in the kitchen. Hopefully the cave drawing of your home will have people with smiles on their faces.

Do you use your garage as a garage or a storage facility?

Garage space is not counted as square footage. The presence of a garage, though, can add a 0–20 percent premium on your real estate, depending on where you live. Men love garages, and buyers identify them as important features in their home purchases, but what do people actually use their garages for?

Not cars.

Stuff.

Most garages are used for storage of everything except cars (the impact of this clutter is covered in chapter 4). Take a second to think of the garage you have or the ones your friends have. If yours is clean and has a car in it, you are atypical.

A second item many families have in their garage is a second refrigerator. Additionally, Americans use the garages for secondary refrigeration stockpiles of frozen food. Are you trading a nice kitchen for a large garage that stores garbage, including frozen food? Are you better off with a carport that you won't fill will junk?

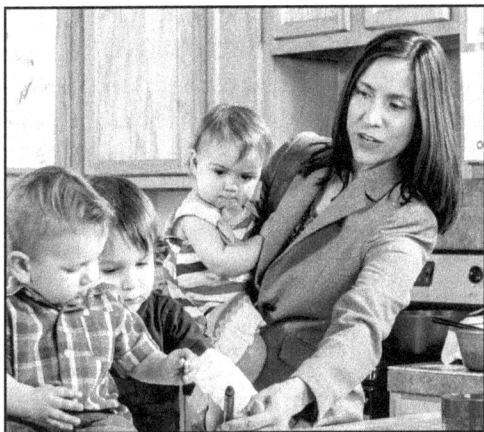

BRINGING IT ALL HOME

On September 1, 2009, I went for a bike ride with a good friend on Vashon Island, near Seattle, Washington. By 7:45 a.m., he was lying on his back, perished, under the silent sweeping arms of Douglas fir trees on the side of the road.

We had taken a ferryboat to Vashon, minutes from downtown Seattle, to get a workout in before a day of tasks. I was to sell real estate; he was to pour a concrete pad on the north side of his home for his son's upcoming wedding.

Within minutes of departing the ferryboat through dense, dramatic Pacific Northwest fog, we had ridden up one hill and halfway down another when my riding partner experienced what I believe was sudden cardiac arrest; he lost control of his bike and fell to his death on a winding country road in the woods.

By 8:30 a.m., the fire department had come and gone; the police had questioned me, and I was alone, on the side of the road, and wishing I was still in bed. Wanting to leave the eerie darkness of the fern-filled forest on that hill, I had no choice but to get back on my bike and start making my way back to the ferry terminal. Sitting on the ferryboat on the ride home, I realized his wife and family probably hadn't been told exactly where and how their husband, father, and grandfather had passed.

"How the heck do I tell his family?" I thought.

I prepared his wife with a succinct phone call and then drove directly to their home, south of Seattle, where his whole family and extended family—probably about fifteen people—were waiting for me. He had owned a commanding Pacific Northwest midcentury modern home on a

Ferry boat, Puget Sound, Washington

large lot, with a sweeping Puget Sound sunset view under the watchful eyes of resident bald eagles. His home was, and still is, physically beautiful, a magazine-worthy estate I would feel lucky to ever own.

I have sold tens of millions of dollars of real estate in my short professional career, but **I learned more about real estate on that day than on any other.**

Though his physical home was the same, the home itself was different after his death and would never be the same. The wood, nails, glass, and cement that fortified his life's work and memories was the same exact structure, but a vastly different one. It would never be the same, for me, and definitely not for his family.

A home, it occurred to me—I was then twenty-eight years old—is a feeling as much as it is a thing. It is an emotion as much as it is a structure.

It's impossible to say exactly what is right and what is wrong in nearly any category humans discuss, including real-estate decisions. There are, though, better and worse choices and better and worse outcomes. We aspire daily to make the better choices for our loved ones, our world, and our personal adventure on this planet. This book was produced to help you make the best choices with regard to your domestic home choice so that you can maximize the wonderful journey you have and to solidify your travel through life as productive, positive, and meaningful.

I wrote this book so that your home can feel as good as it possibly can for you and your loved ones.

Your home has a huge impact on your life.

Both the evidential and scientific information in this book are well researched. Importantly, however, they support my personal experience as a top-producing real-estate salesperson—I have been through the renting, buying, financing, and divorcing processes with thousands of people worth millions of dollars in life-dictating circumstances. Most importantly, I have listened to and watched those whom I consider my many great friends choose homes.

Clearly, at this point, I have a tested opinion about the home-buying decision process. It can be stated in the following five principles:

1. Less is more.
2. People before places.
3. Simplicity beats complexity.
4. Fitness trumps finish level; don't stress over minor design flaws—go have fun.
5. A slow and thoughtful home-buying process yields greater success than a harried and forced one.

There is always another physical home; there is always another piece of construction you can buy. The same is not true for your life; you only get one chance.

I do not and will not profess to know what makes people happy, or even if this is the end goal of life and living. I myself am eccentric with regard to home and lifestyle, and I love my life. **I do hope, sincerely, that this book helped you analyze what is really important to you and how you can set yourself up to get it.**

I am highly interested in hearing about your life-choosing and home-buying process at www.mattcparker.com.

Thank you for reading this book, and good luck with your next home—I know you will enjoy it!

SUGGESTED READING

Arnold, Jeanne E., Anthony P. Graesch, Enzo Ragazzini, and Elinor Ochs. *Life at Home in the Twenty-First Century: 32 Families Open Their Doors.* The Cotsen Institute of Archaeology Press, Los Angeles, CA, July 12, 2012.

Rascoff, Spencer, and Stan Humphries. *Zillow Talk. The New Rules of Real Estate.* Grand Central Publishing, New York, January 27, 2015.

Robert T. Rich *Dad, Poor Dad What the Rich Teach Their Kids About Money—That the Poor and Middle Class Do Not.* Warner Books Ed., New York, NY, 2000.

DEDICATION

To my bride.

ACKNOWLEDGMENTS

For you who read my books, I am very grateful.
May we continue to challenge and inspire each other!

For hours of selfless proofreading, I appreciate HP and KP.

For great help, business coverage, and teamwork I appreciate Tammy, Christy, and Mick.

Here's to freeing your best person, in your best life, in your best home, today.

Thanks to Mario Jannatpour, for mentorship.

Thanks to Adam Restad and Elliot Trotter, for great design work.

www.ingramcontent.com/pod-product-compliance
Lightning Source LLC
Chambersburg PA
CBHW060502280326
41933CB00014B/2830